John Wesley Hanson

Aion-aionios

An Excursus on the Greek Word rendered everlasting, eternal, etc., in the Holy

Bible

John Wesley Hanson

Aion-aionios

An Excursus on the Greek Word rendered everlasting, eternal, etc., in the Holy Bible

ISBN/EAN: 9783337172954

Printed in Europe, USA, Canada, Australia, Japan

Cover: Foto ©ninafisch / pixelio.de

More available books at **www.hansebooks.com**

AIŌN-AIŌNIOS:

AN EXCURSUS ON THE GREEK WORD RENDERED EVER-LASTING, ETERNAL, ETC., IN THE HOLY BIBLE.

With Appendixes.

BY

JOHN WESLEY HANSON, A. M., D. D.

Quanto quis altius eruditione in antiquitate Christiana eminuit, tanto magis, spem finiendorum olim cruciatûm aluit atque defendit.
—J. C. DŒDERLEIN, Inst. Theol. Chr., Vol. II, p. 199.

CHICAGO:
JANSEN, McCLURG, & COMPANY.
1880.

PREFACE.

The author of this volume has carefully sought to present the *usus loquendi* of the word that forms the last line of defence of the doctrine of endless punishment. It was some time since virtually conceded that the human intellect and the human affections protest against the doctrine, but it is yet claimed that the positive declarations of the Bible, and especially that the texts in which the æonian terms are connected with punishment, announce it so distinctly that it must be accepted as the sentiment of the Bible. With as much care and candor as he could command, constantly impelled by the sole desire to ascertain the facts in the biography of the word, the author has traced it from its earliest appearance until it had been in constant use for nearly two thousand years. He has quoted or cited the first hundred or more passages in which it occurs, and has given illustrative instances of its use in each of the more recent centuries, and has referred to most of the texts in the Bible containing it.

In sending out the results of his investigations he asks each of his readers to do him the favor to notify him of any error, however slight, that may possibly be detected, though he dares venture to believe that few or none such will be discovered.

May the book be read with the disposition that has actuated its preparation, and carry conviction only as it conveys the truth!

CHICAGO, JULY, 1880.

CONTENTS.

I. INTRODUCTION 9-16
II. ETYMOLOGY...17-29
III. LEXICOGRAPHY...30-47
IV. USAGE.—I. CLASSIC 48-62
      II. OLD TESTAMENT...62-86
      III. JEWISH GREEK................................86-91
      IV. NEW TESTAMENT 91-146
      V. EARLY CHRISTIAN..............................146-162
APPENDIX A..163
      B 164
      C...166
      D...167

INDEX.

Page.

Abbot, Prof., Harvard Un'y.....158
Acton's definition of *aiŏn* 36
Adialeiptos.......................120
Æi, meaning of,...............24-27
——limited.......................126
——number of times in New Testament.........................25
Æons, doctrine of..............114
Æschylus' use of *aiŏn*.... 34, 49,
..........................52, 58
Agamemnon......................52
Agesilaus......................89, 163
Ages in Bible.............38, 133
Aidios..120. Appendix B, 89, 122
...............164, 124, 125
Aiŏn, a human life 136
——beginning of 98
——Christian life..............94
——Classic use of..............148
——derivation of.............17-29
——end of......................133
——finite duration...............94
——God's endless..........26, 65, 95
——governed by eis..... 140
——Idumea's limited.............26
——in New Testament...39, 99, 100
——Jewish age..................93
——Kingdom of Christ............92
——long time....................94
——man's limited..............26
——more than eternal............99
——New Testament use.39, 92, 100
——Old Testament use...13, 63, 73
——plural........ 94

Page.

Aiŏn, repetitions of.............99
——same as olam.................13
——times in Old Testament.... 65
——usage of..................30, 46
Aiŏnion life and aiŏnion punishment same....................125
Aiŏnion life lost..............129
Aiŏnios in Old Testament......69
——not same in same sentence.117
——punishment in New Test...104
——times in NewTestament 92, 101,
.................................103
Akataluton.................119, 122
Alcestis..........................26
Alcinous..........................51
Alexandrinus, Clemens.........157
Alford...........................138
Alger's Future Life.... 112
Alleged Discrepancies of Bible..
.................................12
Amarantos...............119, 122-25
Amarantinos...........119, 122-25
Ambrose..... 157
Anacreon..........................62
Anderson, Galusha, D. D.......139
Andromache...................49, 52
Anthologica Græca.............164
Anthology.......................163
Anthology, Greek...............163
Ant. Jud. Josephus 87, 88
Aphthartos 119, 122-25
Apeiros 122, 122-25
Aperantos 122-25
Apollodorus....................164

Page.

Apollonius Rhodius............163
Apostles'.Creed...............148
Appendix A..................163
——B.........................164
——C.........................167
——D.........................167
Aquinas, Thos................118
Archæology, Jahn's.......... 86
Arethas......................164
Argonautica.................163
Aristotle, 22, 24, 26, 27, 55-60, 114,
...........................121, 122, 123
——his derivation of aiōn........ 26
——his etymologies............28, 29
——his use of aiōn........18, 22, 24
Aryan origin of aiōn........... 19
Assemanui, Bib. Orient........155
Ateleutetos..................89, 121
Atermon 123
Athanasian 119
Athanatos................89, 122
Atheism, Nat. Hist. of........ 44
Augustin, St.,...115, 118, 125, 126,
................155, 158, 160
Auteurieth 84
Avitus 156
Balfour, Walter 83
Barnes, Albert...............135
Bartlett, Prof. S. C....83, 110, 166
Basilidians..................157
Bass' lexicon................ 22
Beard, Dr. J. R.............. 98
Beausobre.................... 86
Beecher, Dr. Edward, 23, 27, 29, 31,
37, 38, 49, 52, 59, 66, 89, 121, 126,
...........147, 149, 151, 157, 158
Beecher, H. W...............86
Benfey...................... 21
Bengel......................132
Benson...................35, 135
Blackie, Prof. J. S.......... 44
Boise, Dr. J. R......22, 23, 139, 140
Boothroyd................... 35
Bopp........................ 21
Bostra, Titus of.............150
Burthog's Christianity 133
Bush, Prof. George..........124
Buxtorf 12
Byzantinus, Leontius.......... 45
Cæsarius.................... 45
Campbell, Dr. A............. 35, 79
Campbell, Dr. Geo...........109
Carpocratians...............157
Celsus......................136
Christian, early usage........146
Christian Examiner. 18, 32, 52, 64,
.............................130
Christian Union............. 86
Clarke, Dr. Adam, 21, 22, 35, 109
.............................134
——Prof. J. C. 51, 53, 61
CLASSICS, GREEK............. 48
Cleanthes..................25, 26
Clemance....................127
Clement of Alexandria113, 143, 157
Clowes, Dr. T..........7, 9, 10, 74
Cousin...................... 56
Cox, Samuel...............56, 114
Cratylus, Plato's............ 28
Cremer's lexicon............26, 59
Cruden......................35

Page.

Crusius 49
Cu tiu ·...................19, 21
Damascus, John of........... 80
Damm's lexicon.............. 27
De Bello, Josephus'........87, 88
De Cœlo 22, 26, 57
De Humanitate, Philo's....... 89
De Lamennais................ 44
Demarest, Rev. G. L.........124
De Mundo 123
De Pœni, Philo's.............897
De Premiis, Philo's.......... 89
De Quincey, Thos............ 40
Destruction, everlasting....13, 137
De Ver. Grotius............. 18
De Wette.................44, 145
Dexippus....................164
Diaglot, Emphatic, 45, 111, 112,
.............................139
Didymus....................157
Dietelmair..................138
Diodorus...............51, 59, 157
Divine Goodness, Smith's..... 89
Doddridge, Dr............... 86
Doederlein...............155, 159
Dollinger 80
Donelson 21
Donnegan................26, 33, 110
Dorner..................153, 155
Duncan 12
"Dust of the Earth".......... 82
EARLY CHRISTIAN USAGE......146
Edwards, Jonathan...........126
Eis ton aiōna 138, 142, 168
Empedocles...............51, 56
Emphatic Diaglot.45, 111, 112, 139
Encyclopædia Rel. Knowl...... 12
Endlessness, words signifying 119,
.............................122, 125
——never applied to punishment,
.............................123
Endless Punishment, not in Old
Testament................6, 7, 85
Epictetus..............51, 52, 54
Erinna...................52, 61
Erotianus................... 20
Essenes, doctrine of.......88, 123
Eternal Hope.44, 80, 113, 125, 136,
.............................158
Eternity, a modern idea.10, 11, 44
Etymologicum, Ling. Græc..17, 32
ETYMOLOGY................... 17
Etymology no guide........... 28
Eunomius...................166
Euripides.............26, 34, 50-52
Eusebius.................26, 154
Everlasting................. 77
——destruction.............105, 137
——punishment.............105, 137
——damnation............. 78, 105
——fire.....................135
Ewing...................33, 122
Examiner, Christian... 18, 32, 52,
.............................64, 130
——and Chronicle.........53, 57, 60
Exegetical Essays...........103
Expositor, Universalist.......130
Farrar, Canon, 43, 44, 80, 113, 115,
.........116, 125, 131, 136, 145, 158
Ferrar...................21, 44
Fire, everlasting.............135

Page.

Fire, disciplinary.........114, 115
Forever...........77, 139, 145, 137
Foster, John................ 39
Fragmenta, Philo's............ 20
Fragments, Pindar's.......... 20
Furniss.....................126
Fürst and Taylor............ 38
Geikie's Life of Christ.......... 62
Gehenna limited in duration...131
——explained................137
Gesenius................12, 14, 16
Giesel 155
Giles.... 35
Gilpin 35
Goodness, Divine, Smith's 39
Goodwin, Rev. E. S., 18, 32, 52, 54,
................57, 60, 64
Gorgias.................... 56
Gospel of Nicodemus...........155
GREEK CLASSICS.............. 48
——Jewish................. 86
——the language of Jews....... 63
Greenfield..................110
Gregory of Nyssa......116, 117, 158,
................166
——Thaumaturgus............157
Griesbach.................102, 132
Grimm 26
Grote on Plato and Aristotle. 28,
................29
Grotius, De Ver....18, 26, 110, 132
Grove, lexicon.........22, 33, 122
Guericke...................155
Hagenbach.................155
Haley, J. W.............. 12
Hammond................35, 36, 134
Hector...................49, 52
Hedericus............32, 36, 110
Heraclitus.................. 24
Hermas...................158
Hermogenes 150
Herodian 51, 59
Hero lotus..............37, 59
Hesiod...............37, 49
Hesychius............30, 45, 51
Hierocles................. 51
Hincks................... 34
Hippocrates............20, 50
Historia Dogmatis............138
Hodge, Dr................136, 137
Homer..21, 23, 37, 48, 49, 136, 156
Homeric Dictionary.......... 34
Hope, Eternal.......44, 80, 81, 113,
................125, 136, 158
Huetius.................... 45
Huidekoper................138
Hypolitus..................158
Ignatius 148, 158
Iliad........21, 48, 49, 136
Inquiry, Balfour's............ 83
Inter-Ocean................23, 139
INTRODUCTION.............. 9
Irenæus................ 147, 149
Isidore....................157
Isocrates................51, 58
Israelitische Religionslehre....131
Jacob.................... 62
Jahn..... 85
Jerome....................157
Jewish authorities cited........131
JEWISH GREEK.................. 86

Page.

Jews Hellenized............63, 166
——History of................ 86
——opinions of................166
——reject endless punishment,
................131
John of Damascus.............. 30
Jones...................... 35
Josephus' use of aiŏn, 87, 114,
................129, 130
——use of kolasis......110, 111, 114
Judgment, æonian 138
Justinian, Emperor.......121, 123,
................152, 158, 159
Justin Martyr....123, 147, 148, 158
................159
Keble......................118
Kenrick.................... 38
Kingsley, Chas 46, 119
Knapp.................11, 79, 102
Kolasis....................109, 114
Kuhn...................... 21
Kurtz.....................155
Lange..........37, 72, 133, 138, 146
Le Clerc...............11, 36, 79
Leonidas...................164
Leonidas the Alexandrine.....163
Leontius Byzantinus............ 45
LEXICOGRAPHY................. 30
Liddell and Scott....25, 26, 34, 110
Life eternal limited..............129
Lindsay 35
Locke...................... 36
Lucian's Dialogues 26
Lucretius................... 20
Lutz....................34, 36
LXX, meaning of............. 16
Macknight................. 34, 99
Maclaine................... 36
Manetho...................156
Mangey's ed. of Philo 89
Mardon.................... 35
Martyr, Justin.........123, 148, 158
Massuetus.................149
Maurice, F. D................ 46
Meier..................... 13
Melinna 62
Mennas......121, 123, 152, 157 159
Mill......................132
Milman.................... 85
Minucius Felix..............126
Mission to Underworld........138
Modern Universalism, Bartlett's,
.... 84
Mœbius.................... 62
Moody.....................126
Mopsuestia, Theodore of....152-3
Mosheim.............36, 147, 153
Müller, Max.............21, 110
Mundi, Salvator..............114
Murdoch...................147
Neander................30, 155
Never...................... 77
NEW TESTAMENT USAGE... 91
——Testament, when compiled,147
Newton, Sir I............99, 109, 140
Nicene Creed...............147-8
Nicodemus, Gospel of..........155
Noyes, G. R., D. D.............139
Nyssa, Gregory of.........116, 155
Odyssey................21, 48, 49
Olam, derivation of..........10, 13

Page.
——different degrees of.......12, 13
——duration of 10, 13
——Hebrew synonyms of....... 13
——meaning of.........9, 14, 15
——times in Bible.........9, 10
OLD TESTAMENT USAGE....... 62
Olshausen.................. 36, 168
Olympiodorus..........56, 157, 158
On..................... 25
Oppert.................. 19
Oracles, Sibylline... ..148, 153, 160
Orestes................. 52
Origen.............45, 136, 151
Orosius 126
Orphica 149
Paige's Commentary..........134
Paige's Selections..........135
Paley..................85
Parkhurst.............11, 22, 25
Palladius.............157
Parker, Prof. I. N..........150
Passow.............. 33
Paulus................. 36
Pearce..............35, 134
Peile.................. 21
Pentateuch, translated........ 62
Peshito version....... 146-7
Phædon.............. 56
Pharisees, doctrine of......88, 128
Phavorinus...........18, 31
Philipson..............131
Philoctetes............... 50
Philo, his use of Greek words, 89,
..............114, 128, 130
Philo Judæus..........51, 113, 130
Pickering.............34, 36
Pindar..........20, 37, 49, 52
Plato.... 23, 53, 56, 60, 62, 110, 114
——etymologies of............28, 29
Plotinus............. 27
Plumtre, Prof...........114
Plutarch.............51, 52
Polycarp 149, 158
Pott.................. 21
Priam.............. 49
Prideaux............. 62
Prison, spirits in..............138
Proclus 27
Prœp. Evang 26
Prometheus............ 52
Punishment, aiōn........ 81
——aiōnion in New Test...104, 187
——reformatory.......107, 109, 112
Pusey, Dr........ 43, 116, 118, 126
Pythagoras..............122
Rabbinical belief in limited pun-
ishment..................131
Rambach.............. 13
Reed, C. H.............. 22
Robertson............. 12
Robinson..........26, 35, 144
Rosenmüller..............134
Rost................. 32
Ruhnken 20
Salvator Mundi..........114, 170
Sanscrit origin of aiōn......19, 21
Sappho.............61, 62
Sarpedon............. 52
Sayce............. 21
Scarlett..........36, 79

Page.
Schaff..................150
Schindler.............. 12
Schleicher 21
Schleiermacher 21, 29
Schleusner..........33, 37, 79
Schmidt.............. 21
Schrevelius 33, 36
Schweighæuser.......... 35, 36
Sears, Dr. E. H.......... 43
Septuagint.............. 64
Sibylline Oracles..........148
Simpson..............35, 39
Sin Against Holy Ghost..........132
Smith, T. Southwood........36, 39
Socrates................54, 110
Sodom and Gomorrah..........135
Solom. Parab 89
Sophocles..........24, 49, 52, 59
Spirits in Prison..............138
Spurgeon, C. H............126
Stephelin's Rabbins..........131
Stephens, Henry 24, 26, 27, 37
Stephens' Thesausus.......... 89
Stuart, Moses......36, 79, 103, 144
Swing, Prof. David.......... 71
Synonyms, Trench's........20, 113
——of New Test.............. 20
Syriac Version.........11, 146, 148
Taylor and Fürst.............. 38
——Dr.................33, 79
Tennyson 116
Tertullian 126
Theodore of Mopsuestia......152, 3
Theodoret................ 30
Theolog. Zeitschrift..........144
Thesaurus, Robertson's........ 12
——Stephens'.................. 89
Timæus..........52, 53, 55, 57, 60
Times, Chicago..............139
Titus of Bostra..............150
Trench's Synonyms...20, 113, 114
Tribune, Chicago.............. 22
Trypho Dialogue..............148
Union, Christian.......... 86
Universalism, Modern.......... 83
——Anc. Hist.............155
Universalist Book of Ref....... 77
——Expos..............130
Universal Restitution, Three-fold
Basis of..................167
Valpley................35, 36
Wakefield..........35, 109, 134
Warburton.............. 85
Welker.................. 62
Westcott..............147
Wetstein..............102
Whateley 85
Whitby 35
White, Pres. N., 18, 21, 29, 61, 150,
.................155, 156, 163
Whiton, Dr., 14, 101, 121, 127, 136,
.................143, 148, 165
Wilson's Diaglot 45
World, end of 109
Worms, undying 115
Wright................ 35
Xenophon.. ....37, 59, 163
Zehetmayr.............. 20
Zoen aiōnion..............127, 128
Zonar.................. 31

AIŌN-AIŌNIOS.[1]

INTRODUCTION.

The word that is rendered *aiōn-aiōnios*[2] in the Greek Septuagint, and everlasting, eternal, etc., in the English Bible, is *olam*,[3] in the original Hebrew Scriptures, derived from *olm*,[4] to cover, or conceal. It literally means hidden, unknown, and, when applied to time, it signifies indefinite duration, whether past or future.[5] Thus, the hills are said to exist from *olam*. As the Hebrew knew that they had a beginning with the creation of the earth, and would end with its destruction, of course he did not mean to say that the hills are literally everlasting when he termed them olamic. As he knew that they had a beginning, so he knew they would have an end; but as the period of their duration was unknown, he said they were from *olam*. The word is used in one text[6] in both a limited and unlimited sense; and it signifies in one case[7] only three days and three nights.

So of future time, some things were to exist to *olam*, e. g., the Covenant, the Law, the Mosaic Economy, the Levitical Priesthood, etc., though it was supposed they would cease at Messiah's advent. They are *olamic*, because their duration is indefinite, hidden, concealed from man. Dr. T. Clowes observes:—"The word *olam* is used 459 times in the

---

[1] ΑΙΩΝ-ΑΙΩΝΙΟΣ.   [2] αἰών-αἰώνιος.   [3] עוֹלָם   [4] עלם
[5] The lexicons are uniform in giving this definition.
[6] Hab. iii : 6.   [7] Jonah ii : 6.

Old Testament; and when we consider how uniformly the
Septuagint translators and the writers of the New Testament
have rendered the word by *aiōn* and *aiōnios*, there being
probably not ten instances of deviation from this uniformity
by the Septuagint translators, and not so many by the New
Testament writers; and when we consider further, the manifest advantage of this uniformity to those who in former ages
read the Septuagint and the New Testament in their mother
tongue, in giving them a clear and definite idea of *olam*, we
are led to express a deep regret that the English translators
did not give their readers a similar advantage. But our translators have rendered this virtually one word, *olam*, occurring
657 times in the Bible, by almost thirty different words and
phrases; most of them signifying duration, to be sure, but
varying their signification as to its extent from a three days'
duration, to a duration without beginning and without end.
The first five places in which *olam* occurs in the Old Testament are rendered by no less than five different words:—Gen.
iii: 22, *forever;* Gen. vi: 3, *always;* Gen. vi: 4, *of old;* Gen.
ix: 12, *perpetual;* Gen. ix: 16, *everlasting.*" In Gen. xiii:
15, he shows that *olam* signifies the duration of human life,
and remarks:—"And let no one be surprised that we use the
word *olam* in this limited sense.   This is one of the most
usual significations of the Hebrew *olam* and the Greek *aiōn*,
and it is perfectly right to use Scripture terms in Scripture
senses. This sense of *olam* and *aiōn* runs through all the
writers in Greek, Latin and English. . . .   There is no
evidence that any words in the Old Testament implying duration refer to the future life of man. Neither is it certain
that the ancients, by the terms of duration which they
employed to describe the Divine existence, fully comprehended the idea of interminable existence.   Indeed,
this is an idea beyond the reach of any human intelli-
gence. The Hebrew spoke of the earthly existence of man
as his *olam*. The Greeks and Latins had the same manner
of speaking. The *aiōn* or *ævum* of man, meant the period
of his existence, consisting of a few years on earth; the *aiōn*

or *ævum* of God conveyed the idea of existence without beginning of years or end of life." Parkhurst says:—"It denotes a hidden duration, and it seems to be used much more frequently for indefinite, than for infinite time."

If the ancient Hebrew wished to express great but unknown duration, past or future, he resorted to reduplications and intensified forms, as in Micah[8]:—"We will walk in the name of the Lord our God for an *olam* and an *olam* of *olams*," according to the Syriac version[9], or, in the Hebrew, for an *olam* of *ads*,—the latter word being a synonym of the former. The phrases, "generations of *olams*," and "*olams* of *ads*," are intensified forms of the word for the purpose of describing indefinite, but still limited, duration; for at the time the Old Testament was written the Hebrew mind had not cognized the metaphysical idea of endless duration, and therefore could have no word expressive of eternity. Says a French author[10]: —"It is certain that in the Hebrew there is no word which, properly speaking, signifies eternity or a time which has no end. *Gnolam* signifies only a time, of which we know not the beginning or the end; according to the signification of its root, which means to conceal, to hide. Thus it is to be understood more or less strictly according to the object to which it is applied. When it relates to God or his attributes we should take it in its largest possible extent, that is to say, of an absolute eternity. But when it is applied to things that have a beginning or an end, we must understand it in a manner so limited as the subject requires. Thus, when God says of the Jewish laws that they should be observed *le gnolam*, forever, we must understand a space of time as long as God should find it proper, a space of which the Jews, before the coming of the Messiah, did not know the end." An equally eminent German writer[11] declares:—"The pure idea of eternity is too abstract to have been conceived in the early ages of the world,

---

[8] iv: 5. [9] Tayler Lewis in Lange's Commentary.

[10] LeClerc, 1705. (*Olam* is here spelled after the French and Portuguese fashion, the *g* being silent.) [11] Knapp, Greek Testament.

and accordingly is not found expressed by any word in the
ancient languages.   But as cultivation advanced and this idea
became more distinctly developed, it became necessary in order
to express it to invent new words in a new sense, as was done
with the words *eternitas, perennitas,* etc. The Hebrews
were destitute of any single word to express endless duration.
To express a past eternity they said, before the world was; a
future, when the world shall be no more.   .   .   .   The
Hebrews and other ancient people have no one word for
expressing the precise idea of eternity." To render *olam*
by eternal or everlasting, is therefore manifestly incorrect, or
to translate its intensified forms by forever, forever and ever,
etc., is equally inaccurate. The exact equivalent of the noun
olam is age, epoch, æon. The double form of *aiōn* is a rendering of the Hebrew *olam va ad. Olam* is long time, *olam va
ad*, longer time. But if *olam* were eternity, to affix words
denoting longer would be absurd. In the Septuagint *ton
aiōna, kai ep' aiōna, kai eti,* and in the New Testament *eis
tous aiōnas tōn aiōnōn,* etc., are Greek equivalents of *olam
va ad,* meaning literally, in English, long, but limited duration.

Duncan, in his Hebrew Lexicon, thus defines *olam:*—1.
"A long indefinite period. *Tempus homini absconditum
tam infinitum et eternum quam finitum, ut* Gen. xvii: 8,
etc., *plerumque est perpetuum, eternum, sempiternum.*
Robertson's Thesaurus. Exod. xxi: 6.—2. Perpetuity, dura-
bility, Is. lxiv: 4.—But most frequently eternity.—3. The
world, Eccles. iii: 11." Buxtorf and Schindler define *olam* as
"A hidden time, an age, time hidden from man." "Gesenius, in the last edition of his Hebrew Lexicon, gives
eternity as the first meaning of *olam,* but remarks that "it is
frequently used in a limited sense.[12]" J. W. Haley asserts[13]
that "the Hebrew *olam,* rendered forever, does not imply
the metaphysical idea of absolute endlessness, but a period

[12] Encyclopædia of Religious Knowledge. p. 53.
[13] Alleged Discrepancies of the Bible, p. 126.

of indefinite length, as Rambach says, " a very long time, the end of which is hidden from us."

Of course the Greek word *aiōn* into which the Hebrew *olam* is almost always rendered, must, in the Old Testament, have the precise meaning of the word it represents; and all the modifications of *aiōn*, its reduplications and intensified forms, must carry the same force as do the Hebrew expressions whence they are derived. As from *olam* signifies from an indefinite past time, and to *olam* an unknown time in the future, to be interpreted by the subject treated, so from an *aiōn* or to an *aiōn*, must denote indefinite time. An olamic period is an aionian period, and an *olam* of *olams* or an *olam* of *ads* is an age of ages. It follows that the corresponding Greek form *eis tous aiōnas tōn aiōnōn*, instead of being rendered forever, or forever and ever, should in English, be represented by an age of ages, or ages of ages, or some other phrase indicating an indefinite period to be determined by the subject treated. Of their own intrinsic force the words cannot denote endless duration.[14]

The "Comparative Hebrew Lexicon" of Meier says that *olam* (as a verb) is derived from *olaph*, to cover, to conceal, to hide away. He also gives as the meaning of *olam* (as a noun), undetermined (or indefinite) time, past or future,— hence, remote time and eternity; thus averring that *eternity* is not the original but the derived meaning. He gives also as a later meaning *time, timehood*, (German, *zeitlichkeit*). Besides, he says that *zeitlichkeit* also means world.

---

[14] It may be observed that there are several other words that are sometimes used as the equivalents of *olam: ad*, until ; *netsach*, flowing ; *tamid*, stationary ; *dor*, generation ; *kedem*, east ; *kol yamim*, all days ; *orek*, long ; *yamim*, days ; *adi-ad*, to long future time ; *la-ad*, to long future time ; *dor vador*, generation to generation. We give the literal meaning, but they are employed to indicate indefinite duration. If *olam* meant eternity, it would be absurd to try to add to its meaning by saying *olam va ad; if aiōn* meant eternity, it would be equally absurd to say *eis ton aiōna, kai eis ton aiōna*, etc., in the Old Testament, or *eis tous aiōnas tōn aiōnōn* in the New Testament. No rule of language would permit their use. But as the nouns simply denote a long time, it is proper to extend their meaning.

It has long been a prevalent opinion that the words forever, everlasting, eternal, and their cognates in the English
Bible, signify endless duration, because it has been supposed
that the Hebrew and Greek words from which they are rendered
have that meaning, and, as they are found qualifying punishment, it is believed that the occurrence of the words in
such a connection demonstrates the endlessness of punishment. The author of this treatise has endeavored to put
within brief compass the essential facts pertaining to the
history and use of the word, and he thinks he conclusively
shows that it does not afford any support whatever to the erroneous doctrine. It will generally be conceded that this tenet
is not contained in the Scriptures if the meaning of
endless duration does not reside in the controverted word.
The reader is implored to examine the evidence presented, as
the author trusts it has been collected, with a sincere desire
to learn the truth. The inquiry is pursued in a manner
intended to be satisfactory to the scholar, while it shall also
be within the apprehension of the ordinary reader, so that
the learned and the unlearned may be able to see the subject
in a light that shall relieve the Scriptures of seeming to teach
a doctrine that blackens the character of God, and plunges
a deadly sting into the believing heart.

It is not going too far to say that if the word in question
does not carry the force of endless duration, then the dogma
of endless punishment is not found in the Bible. This
excursus shows that interminable duration does not reside in
the word.[15]

---

[15] While passing this work through the press, we came across the following on "*olam*" in Appendix A, in Is Eternal Punishment Endless? by Rev.
J. M. Whiton :

"GESENIUS'S HEBREW-ENGLISH LEXICON,—'OLAM.

"A) Properly 'hidden,' specially *hidden time, i. e.,* obscure and long, of
which the beginning or end is uncertain or indefinite, *duration, everlasting,
eternity,* spoken :

"1. Of time *long past,* gray antiquity, as Gen. vi : 4, mighty men which
were *of old* (from '*olam*.)

"2. Often also of *future* time, *ever, forever,* in such a way that the limitation is to be determined from the nature of the subject, Thus,

"a) Specially in the affairs of single persons, '*olam* is sometimes put for the whole period of life, as, *a servant forever* (of '*olam*), *i. e.*, not to be set free in all his life (Deut. xv:17). Sometimes put for *very long life*, (Ps. xxi:4) *length of days for ever and ever* ('*olam va'ed* [like our *for ever and aye*]).

"b) As pertaining to a whole race, dynasty, or people, and including *the whole time* of their existence until their destruction. I Sam. ii:30, *Thy family shall serve me forever* (to '*olam*), *i. e.*, so long as it endures.

"c) Nearer to the *metaphysical* notion of *eternity*, or at least to an eternity without end, approach those examples in which '*olam* is attributed to the earth and to the universe. Eccl. i:4, *the earth abideth forever* (for '*olam*). So of human things which refer to a period after death, *e. g.*, sleep of '*olam*, *everlasting sleep*, for death, Jer. li:39, 57; house of '*olam*, his *everlasting house*, long home, Eccl. xii:5.

"d) The true and full idea of *eternity* is expressed by '*olam* in those passages where it is spoken of the nature and existence of God, who is called, (Gen. xxi:33), the *God of* '*olam*. Of him it is said (Ps. xc:2), *from* '*olam and unto* '*olam Thou art God*.

"e) Of a peculiar kind are those passages where the Hebrews by hyperbole ascribe *eternity* in the metaphysical sense to human things, chiefly in the expression of good wishes; *let my lord the king live forever* (to '*olam*), I Kings i:31.

"PLUR. '*olamim, ages, everlasting ages*, like Gr. αἰῶνες [*æons*], *i. e.*, a) *ages of antiquity*, Is. li:9; b) *future ages*, the remotest future, Ps. lxxvii:7.

"B) *The World*, like Gr. αἰών [*æon*], hence *love of worldly things, worldly-mindedness*. So Eccl. iii:11, *Although he* (God) *hath set the love of worldly things* ('*olam*) *in their heart, so that man understandeth not the works of God*. [So in the New Testament, '*Be not conformed to this world*' (*æon*—Romans xii:2), is equivalent to '*Love not the world*' (*cosmos*— I John ii:15).]"

It would seem unnecessary to suggest that limited duration is the prevailing sense of this word by an immense preponderance. Dr. Whiton observes, also, pp. 9-10:

"'*Olam* in the Hebrew Testament very frequently meant a *world-period* or *cycle*.

"Ecclesiastes i:4—The earth abideth forever, literally, for the '*olam*, or *cycle*: LXX. for the *æon*.

"Psalm cxlv:13—Thy kingdom is an everlasting kingdom; literally, a kingdom of all '*olams*, or cycles; LXX. of all the *æons*.

"Exodus xl:15—Their anointing shall surely be for an everlasting priesthood; literally, for a priesthood of '*olam*, or a cycle; LXX. a priestly anointing for the *æon*.

"In this last instance, the '*olam*, cycle, or *æon*, closed, as we see by comparing Hebrews vii:11, 12, at the end of the Mosaic dispensation.

"Again.

"Psalm cxliii:3—Those that have been long dead; literally, the dead of '*olam*, or, as we should say, "the dead of ages;" LXX. the dead of *æon*.

"The word *æon* accordingly retains in the New Testament this peculiar Hebraistic color which the LXX. had given to it."

[The unlearned reader should understand by LXX., the Greek Old Testament, that is, the Septuagint, translated from the Hebrew by seventy scholars, hence called the LXX.]

Three avenues are open to us through which to pursue this important investigation:—I. ETYMOLOGY; II. LEXICOGRAPHY; III. USAGE.

ETYMOLOGY.

In studying a controverted word it is interesting to ascertain, if possible, its derivation, though there can be no more unsafe and treacherous guide to the meaning of words than Etymology. Usage is the only unerring index. Etymology is hypothesis; usage is demonstration. Thus, our common word *prevent* is derived from *præ* and *venio*, to come or go before, and originally the English word prevent signified to go before, as in the Psalm,[1] "In the morning shall my prayer *prevent* thee"; but the word long since changed its meaning to hinder. Suppose two thousand years hence some one should endeavor to prove that in the year 1880 the word prevent meant to go before. He could easily establish his position by the etymology of the word, but he would be wholly wrong, as would appear by universal usage in our current literature. So that if we agree that the etymology of *aiōn* indicates eternity to have been its original meaning, it by no means follows that it has that force in Greek literature, profane or sacred.

The most natural derivation of *aiōn*, however, does not give to the word the sense of endless duration. Lennep[2] says that it comes from *aō* (to breathe) which suggests the idea of indefinite duration. He says:—"It was transferred from breathing to collection, or multitude of times. From which proper signification again have been produced those by which the ancients have described either age (*œvum*), or eternity (*œternitatem*,) or the age of man (*hominis œtatem*).

---

[1] lxxxviii: 13. [2] Etymologicum Linguæ Græcæ.

2

Commenting on Lennep's derivation of the word, Rev. E. S. Goodwin says:[3]—"It would signify a multitude of periods or times united to each other, duration indefinitely continued. Its proper force, in reference to duration, seems to be more that of uninterrupted duration than otherwise; a term of which the duration is continuous as long as it lasts, but which may be completed and finished, as age, dispensation, sæculum, in a general sense." Mr. Goodwin well remarks,[4] "It is not necessary to form *aiōn* by a composition of *aei* and *ōn*. It may arise much more naturally and more in the common order of things, from the verb *aiō*. It need only be its present active participle converted into a substantive, according to a common usage of the Greek language. If applied to breath, it would signify a multitude of breathings, or breathing indefinitely extended; and if applied to simple existence, it would signify existence indefinitely extended." Other scholars suggest *aia*, the *earth*, or *world*, and *ōn*, a participle of *eimi*, to *exist*, as its source.

We submit the following derivation of *aiōn*, to which we invite the scrutiny of scholars:—In Greek a noun with accented omega (long o) in the last syllable of the nominative case singular, signifies a container; that is, the *ōn* indicates that the preceding syllable is contained in it. Thus, a Greek's *loutr-ōn* is his bath-place; a *dendr-ōn* is his grove-place; a *rhod-ōn* is his rose-place, etc. An *aiōn* is, therefore, something that contains an *aei*, or *aia*—a something containing the earth, *aia*; or duration, *aei*; or breathings, *aō*; existence, life;—duration, signified by breathings, is perhaps the best etymology of the word.

President N. White, Ph.D.,[5] of Lombard University, Illinois,

---

[3] Christian Examiner, Vol. X., p. 42. He quotes the ancient Phavorinus as defining it thus: "The comprehension of many times or periods."

[4] Christian Examiner, Vols. X., XI., XIII.

[5] For valuable assistance on this point, we are indebted to President N. White, Ph. D., of Lombard University, Galesburg, Ill., who, when this book first appeared, had already accumulated a large amount of material for a similar work.

one of the best philologists living, has placed us under obligations by furnishing the following etymological description of
the word, tracing it back to remote periods, far antecedent to
its appearance in the Greek language.

The genesis of αἰών seems to be the despair of etymol-
ogists. We have neither time nor space to enter into a de-
tailed discussion of the particular points on which philologists
differ, nor is such discussion needed to obtain a tolerably correct notion of the primitive meaning of the word. Passing
by the absurd views and discussions of the old school of philologists, we shall attempt to present, in the briefest possible
way, the best results of the most eminent of comparative philologists of the present day, respecting this word, so replete
with historical and moral interest.

We begin, then, with the *supposititious* form of the old
Aryan, or mother-tongue, whence αἰών is derived. Here the
ground-form of this word appears as the verbal root, *i*, to go.
This root, by a process called strengthening, (in Sanscrit
vṛiddhi), becomes *ái*. This strengthened form takes the suffix,
-*van*-. Now, if the suffix *vat* be, as suggested by Oppert,[6]
but another form of -*van*- then the *original signification*
of the suffix will be, *he that*, and the complete form *ai-van-*
will mean (since the word is of the masculine gender), *he that
moves* or *goes*; since *va* originally meant "*is, ea, id,*" and -*t*
(the residuum of the demonstrative pronoun *ta*), *this* or *that*.
It may be remarked that the Gothic *ai-va* (in the nominative
masculine *aivs*) closely resembles the hypothetical *ai-van*.

In the Sanscrit *éva-s* we have (speaking chronologically), the oldest form in which the word actually occurs in
written language. Here the secondary suffix *ta* seems to be
supplanted by the gender sign -*s*, which is doubtless a residuum of the Sanscrit third personal pronoun.

The meaning of *éva-s* in the Sanscrit is (logically) removed but a step from the original signification of the word
in the old Aryan. Curtius gives as the meaning in the singular,

---

[6] Sanscrit Gram. p. 233.

"course," "conduct," and in the plural, "custom," "manners."
Zehetmayr agrees with Curtius.[7] It is evident, also, that
Trench regards this meaning as inherent in the Greek αἰών,
since he has made it the basis of his excellent remarks upon
the word.[8]

It is an interesting fact that, philologically speaking, *aevum*
the form which the word assumes in Latin, is older than the
Greek αἰών. *Aevu-m* (later form of *aevo-m*) is clearly the Latin
representative of the neuter of the Sanscrit *éva - s*, the *é* taking
(as usual) the form *ae*.

The original signification of the word in Latin seems to
be "life", "time of life;" it sometimes means "old age."[9] It
may not be out of place to remark that "*per aevom*," in Lucretius,[10] is often quoted as signifying endless duration. An
acquaintance with the views of Lucretius, as well as a careful reading of the context, will show, we think, that the expression cannot so be interpreted. Besides, Lucretius is
comparatively a late writer.

The form in which this word appears in Greek need not
now detain us long. In the ante-classical period of Grecian
literature it was undoubtedly written αἰϜών. Referring
again to the Indo-European, or supposititious *ai-va-n*, it will
suffice to say that the Greek αι - is the undoubted representative of the old *ai-*,—that the digamma Ϝ represents the *v* of
the old Aryan—that the ω is the proper representative of *á*
(long) in the primitive speech, and that the Greek *ν* is the
old *n*. It would seem, then, that the original signification of
αἰών, certainly the signification which best accords with the
etymology, is the "principle of life," or "the strength of life."
In this sense it occurs in Pindar,[11] where αἰών δὲ δι ὀστέων is
rendered by Ruhnken *medulla per ossa diffusa*, i. e., the
marrow. Erotianus[12] defines αἰών as ὁ νωτιαῖος μυελός, or "the
spinal marrow."

---

[7] Lex. Etymol., p. 12.   [8] Syn. N. T., Vol. II., pp. 35, 6.
[9] Eun. in Gell. 12., 2, 3; Plin. Pan. 78. 2. etc.
[10] I. 952, Bernaysius's ed.   [11] Fragments, 77, Donaldson's ed.
[12] Glossary of Hippocrates.

Reminding the reader that we speak logically and not chronologically, we may say that the word is used by Homer in a less primitive sense than in Pindar, or in Hippocrates. In the Iliad and the Odyssey it occurs in the sense of "human life," "time of life," etc., as scores of passages abundantly attest.

We have only space to add that Pott, Benfey, and some other philologists, would connect αἰών with the Sanscrit *áy-us* or *áj-us*, which means, as an adjective, "living," as a masculine substantive, (pronounced oxytone), "man"; and when pronounced baritone, "time of life." [13] Since, however, most philologists agree in referring both *é-va-s* and *áy-us* to the primitive root *i*, any discussion of the etymology of the latter may be pronounced unnecessary. [14]

As we have already observed, the etymology of the word is not decisive in determining its meaning, but this learned exposition by President White will deeply interest the scholar. It reënforces and confirms our theory that continuous but limited, or indefinite duration, is the grammatical, etymological and logical signification of the word.

And yet Dr. Adam Clarke says "there is no word which more forcibly points out the grand characteristic of eternity, . . . endless is its grammatical meaning, and all others are accommodated." This dictum, once apparently accurate, is now seen to be contradicted by the etymology of the word, by the lexicons, which give endless as only one of many meanings, and as we shall subsequently show, by the general usage of

---

[13] Etymol. Vol. II., p. 481.

[14] The reader who wishes to form independent conclusions on the etymology and primitive meaning of αἰών may consult the following works, viz:—Ferrar's Comp. Gram. of Sanscrit, Greek and Latin, pp. 179, 198, *et passim;* Curtius' Greek Etymology, *passim;* Schleicher's Compendium der Vergl.Grammatik der Indogermanischen Sprachen, pp. 398-9 *et passim;* Pott's Etymologische Forschungen, Vol. II., 2., p. 442; Benfey's Griechisches Wurzellexicon,Vol.I., p. 8; Schmidt's Synonymik der Griech. Spr.,Vol. II., p. 54, ff; Bopp's Glossarium Comparativum Linguae Sanscritae, pp. 37, 41; Kuhn's Zeitschrift für Vergl. Sprachforschung, Vol. II., p. 232, ff; and the works of Max Müller, Donelson, Peile, Sayce, and many others.

the word. Dr. Clarke follows the generally received etymology of the word, as it has been supposed that Aristotle gives it, who has been thought to have derived it from a combination of *aei ōn, always-existing.*[15] As there has been no little controversy on this famous passage, we will give the original and three translations. Aristotle says:[16]

Φανερὸν ἅμα ὅτι οὔτε τόπος, οὔτε κενὸν, οὔτε χρόνος ἐστὶν ἔξωθεν. διόπερ οὔτ᾽ ἐν τόπῳ τἀκεῖ πέφυκεν, οὔτε χρόνος αὐτὰ ποιεῖ γηράσκειν, οὐδ᾽ ἐστὶν οὐδενὸς οὐδεμία μεταβολὴ τῶν ὑπὸ τὴν ἐξωτάτω τεταγμένων φοράν, ἀλλ᾽ ἀναλλοίωτα καὶ ἀπαθῆ, τὴν ἀρίστην ἔχοντα ζωὴν καὶ τὴν αὐταρκεστάτην διατελεῖ τὸν ἅπαντα αἰῶνα· καὶ γὰρ τοῦτο τοὔνομα θείως ἔφθεγκται παρὰ τῶν ἀρχαίων. τὸ γὰρ τέλος τὸ περιέχον τὸν τῆς ἑκάστου ζωῆς χρόνον, οὗ μηδὲν ἔξω κατὰ φύσιν, αἰὼν ἑκάστου κέκληται. κατὰ τὸν αὐτὸν δὲ λόγον καὶ τὸ τοῦ παντὸς οὐρανοῦ τέλος, καὶ τὸ τὸν πάντων ἄπειρον χρόνον χαὶ τὴν ἀπειρίαν περιέχον τέλος, αἰών ἐστιν, ἀπὸ τοῦ ἀεὶ εἶναι εἰληφὼς τὴν ἐπωνυμίαν, ἀθάνατος καὶ θεῖος.

Professor J. R. Boise, D.D., LL.D., Professor of Greek in Morgan Park Theological Institution, gives this translation of the passage:[17]

"It is plain, therefore, that there is neither space, nor void nor time beyond. Wherefore, the things there are not by nature in space, nor does time make them grow old, nor is there any change in any one of those things placed beyond the outermost sweep (or current); but, unchangeable and without passion, having the best and most sufficient life, they continue through all eternity (*aiōn*); for this name (i. e., *aiōn*) has been divinely uttered by the ancients. For the definite period (*to telos*), which embraces the time of the life of each individual, to whom, according to nature, there can be nothing beyond, has been called each one's eternity (*aiōn*). And, by parity of reasoning, the definite period also of the entire heaven, even the definite period embracing the infinite

---

[15] Bass, Greek and Eng. Lex., London, 1820; Grove, Greek and Eng. Dict., Boston, 1833; Parkhurst, Greek and Eng. Lex., London, 1822, and Dr. A. Clarke, follow Aristotle.

[16] De Cœlo lib. I. c. 9. [17] Chicago Tribune, 1874, quoted by C. H. Reed.

time of all things and infinity, is an eternity (*aiōn*), immortal and divine, having received the appellation (eternity, *aiōn*) from the fact that it exists always (*apo tou aei einai*)." The reader of this translation is able to see how easily the scholar may be lost in the theologian. Prof. Boise insists that *aiōn* means eternity, and yet he is forced to apply it to a human life, which Aristotle expressly says is one's *aiōn !*

Indeed, we cannot read this translation without perceiving that a pre-conceived theory so colors the author's philological judgment, as to render his statements the speculations of a theologian wedded to a system, rather than the judicial utterances of a Greek scholar, anxious solely for the truth. To say that *aiōn* in this passage should be rendered eternity, is, as this volume will demonstrate to the least learned reader, entirely contrary to the fact.

Dr. Edward Beecher gives the following translation [19] of the controverted sentence:—"On the same principle, the boundaries of all the heavens, and the boundary that incloses and comprehends all time and space, is *aiōn*, a continuous existence, immortal and divine, deriving its name from ἀεὶ εἶναι, to exist continuously." He adds:—"From the time of Homer to Plato and Aristotle, about five centuries, the word *aiōn* is used by poets and historians alongside of various compounds of *aei;* but it is never spelled as if it were a compound of *aei*, for the compounds of *aei* retain the diphthong *ei*, but *aiōn* drops the *e*. There is a verb *aiō*—to breathe, to live. The passage of Aristotle in which his etymology occurs has been mistranslated, for it does not give the etymology of the abstract idea eternity, but of the concrete idea God, as an ever-existing person, from whom all other personal beings derived existence and life. What Aristotle has been supposed to assert of *aiōn*, in the sense of eternity, he asserts of *aiōn* in the sense of God, a living and divine person. That the word *aiōn* in classic Greek sometimes denotes God, is dis-

18 Chicago Inter-Ocean, Jan., 1878.   19 History Fut. Ret., p. 130.

tinctly stated in Henry Stephens' great lexicon (Paris edition), and the passage referred to in Sophocles[20] fully authorizes his statement. In that passage Jupiter is called '*Aiōn*, (the living God,) the Son of Kronos.' Moreover, the whole context of Aristotle proves that he is speaking of the great immovable first mover of the universe, the *Aiōn*, immortal and divine."

This view of the language is a reasonable one, and certainly an accurate rendering of Aristotle's language does not give any color to the common view of Aristotle's meaning. To show that this is true we will give a literal translation of the passage:—"It is, therefore, evident that there is no space, vacuum or time beyond [the heaven]. Wherefore, the things there are unadapted to space, nor does time age them; and they are placed beyond the utmost sweep of change; and changeless, passionless, they, having the best and sufficient life, remain through all duration (*aiōn*), for truly this word was divine according to the ancients. For the completeness which comprehends the time of each one's life, to which, according to nature, there is nothing beyond, has been called his being (*aiōn*). For the same reason the completeness of the whole heaven, even the infinite completeness of all things, and the period including that infinity, is also an *aiōn*, deriving its name from *aei einai*, continual being, immortal, divine."

This passage from Aristotle is obscure, and if he were authority it would not settle the question of the meaning of the word. If we adopt the theory that *aiōn* had the primary meaning of continuous existence, such being the signification of *aei* and *ōn*, there is no warrant even in such an origin for ascribing to it duration without end. But Aristotle does not say or intimate that the word had the meaning of eternity in his day, nor does his statement of its derivation prove that it had that meaning then. On the contrary, Aris-

---

[20] Herac. 900.

totle's use of the word, as we show clearly,[21] proves that it had
no such meaning in his mind, even if it is compounded of *aei*
and *ōn*. Thus *ōn*, being, from *eimi*, to be, and *aei*, from *a*
intensive, and *eo*, to be:—*a* augments, and has the force of
very. *Aei*, long period, and *ōn* only adds being to it. Etymologically, long time is the utmost force of *aei*. Parkhurst
says, "*Aei* signifies (1) *always*, as Acts, vii: 51; II Cor. vi: 10.
(2) *Always, ever*, in restrained sense, as in Mark xv: 8. (3) Very
frequently *continually*, as in I Pet. iii: 15; II Pet. i: 12. The
sense of *ōn* is easily ascertained. In John ix: 25, 'being (*ōn*)
blind.' John viii: 47, 'is (*ōn*) of God.' John xviii: 37, 'is
(*ōn*) of the truth.' *On* denotes simple being or existence."
The sense of *eimi* is equally easy to learn. In John vii: 33,
it is rendered am; also in Matt. xviii: 20, and I Cor. ix: 1.
Aei in II Cor. vi: 10, and Acts vi: 10, is mere continuity. It
is impossible to evolve endless duration from the word. Indefinite duration, determined by the connection, is the utmost
meaning, etymologically.

The word *aei*, from which *aiōn* is claimed to grow, is
found eight times in the New Testament, and in no one instance does it mean endless.[22] We give two texts. The multitude desired Pilate to release a prisoner, Mark xv: 8, "As he
had *ever* done with them." Heb. iii: 10, "They do *always*
err in their heart." An endless duration growing out of a
word used thus would be a curiosity. It is alway or always,
or ever, in each text. Liddell and Scott give more than fifty
compounds of *aei*. Now, if *aiōn* depends on *aei* as its first
member, the meaning must necessarily be limited duration.
In the eight times of its occurrence in the New Testament it
has not the remotest reference to endless duration.

Cleanthes, the poet, in a hymn to Jove, sings, "For thus
thou hast united the good with the evil in one scheme, that
one *constant* principle of reason may be in all, whence those

---

[21] See Classic Usage.
[22] Mark xv: 8; Acts vii: 51; II Cor. iv: 2; vi: 10; Titus i: 12; Heb. iii: 10;
I Pet. iii: 15; II Pet. i: 12.

among mortals who are wicked, ill-starred, are endeavoring to escape, because, indeed, *continually* coveting the property of the good, they neither obey the common law of God, nor listen to it; by obeying it they might enjoy a happy existence with you."[23] Eusebius[24] declares that the darkness preceding creation was infinite, and had no limit for a *long time*, (*polun aiōna*).

Three times it is used in the Alcestis of Euripides, and fourteen times in the Dialogues of Lucian, without denoting endless in a single instance. In Aristotle *aei* occurs thus:[25]

Αἰθέρα προσωνόμασαν τὸν ἀνωτάτω τόπον, ἀπὸ τοῦ θεῖν ἀεὶ τὸν ἀίδιον χρόνον, θέμενοι τὴν ἐπωνυμίαν αὐτῷ.

Thus "the highest Æther," which runs on "continuously," (*aei*) needs "eternal time" (*aïdion kronon*) attached to it to give it the meaning of everlasting; *aei*, as Aristotle understood the word, being inadequate to convey that meaning.

Concerning Aristotle's famous sentence, "Life, an *aiōn* continuous and eternal," it is enough to say that if *aiōn* intrinsically meant endless, Aristotle never would have sought to strengthen its meaning by adding "continuous" and "eternal," any more than one would say, God has an eternity continuous and endless. He has a life, an existence, i. e., an *aiōn*, endless, just as man's *aiōn* on earth is limited; just as Idumea's smoke in the Old Testament is *aiōnios*. Nor, had Aristotle considered *aiōn* to mean eternity, would he have said in this very passage, "the time of the life of each individual has been called his *aiōn*." Cremer, Liddell and Scott, Donnegan, and Henry Stephens adopt the Aristotleian origin of the word. Grimm rejects it, and Robinson in his latest

---

[23] 'Ωδὲ γὰρ εἰς ἕν πάντα συνήρμοκας ἐσθλὰ κακοῖσιν
'Ωσθ' ἕνα γίγνεσθαι πάντων λόγον αἰὲν ἐόντα·
'Ον φείγοντες ἐῶσιν, ὅσοι θνητῶν κακοισί εἰσι,
Δίσμοροι, οἵτ' ἀγαθῶν μὲν ἀεὶ κτῆσιν ποθέοντες,
Οὔτ' ἐσορῶσι θεοῦ κοινὸν νομον, οὔτε κλίουσιν,
'Ω κεν πειθόμενοι σὺν νῷ βίον ἐσθλὸν ἔχοιεν.

[24] Præp. Evang. lib. I. cap. 10. See Grotius, De. Verit. lib. I.
[25] DeCœlo, lib. I. c. 3.

edition gives both etymologies without deciding between them. Stephens says:—"Aristotle, and after him many other philosophers, as Plotinus and Proclus, introduced the etymology of *aiōn* from *aei*, and thus *added* the idea of eternity to the word." Damm, in his "Lexicon and Virtual Concordance of Homer," gives the meaning of *aei* thus:—"Ever, always, perpetually, constantly. It does not always denote duration to infinity, but often continuity of action in a small space of time, or assiduous and earnest action in a limited time, or frequent, or oft-repeated, or habitual action. Often *aei* is completed on the same day." . . *Aiōn* "denotes properly the whole duration of the life of man, the duration of mortal life. Hence, to finish one's *aiōn* is to die. The words *aei ōn* denote existing perpetually, and without any intermission, *until the end comes*."

Beecher observes,[26] "If the etymology of Aristotle were to be accepted, it is not at all decisive of the question; for the word *aei* does not always or even commonly denote or imply eternity. Any careful study of the word *aei* will show that, singly or in compounds, it does not always denote or even imply eternity, but more frequently continuity of being. . . . . It was Pilate's usage to release yearly unto the Jews one prisoner. The mob, therefore, desired him to do as he had ever (*aei*) done unto them, not to or from eternity, but as an annual usage."

But we may hold with Dr. Beecher that the famous passage in Aristotle refers to God (*apo tou aei einai*) and not to abstract duration. We have shown that *aei* is never used in the sense of endless. We shall prove that Aristotle himself uniformly used the word in the sense of limited duration, and, under the head of Classic Usage, will hereafter prove that at the time the Old Testament was rendered into Greek, this was the only meaning the word had with every Greek writer. If *aei ōn* is its source, which is more than doubtful, it cannot mean more than continuous existence, the precise length

<hr />

to be determined by accompanying words. Adopt either derivation, and indefinite duration is the easy and natural etymological meaning. Eternity can only be expressed by it when it is accompanied by other words, carrying the meaning of endless duration, as the name of Deity.

All will agree that words may change their meaning, and therefore that etymology is at best an uncertain guide. If etymology point in one direction, and usage in another, the former must yield; but if both utter one fact, each reënforces and strengthens the other. This we have illustrated by the etymology of *prevent*. Hundreds of words teach the same truth. Words start out with certain meanings, and change in process of time. If *aiōn* really meant eternity when it was first pronounced, it would not follow that it had this meaning later. That it had not that meaning at first would not hinder it from being thus used subsequently. Etymology proves nothing one way or the other—its evidence is but *prima facie*. But etymology gives no warrant for applying the idea of eternity to the word.

Many critics have proceeded on the ground that Aristotle's etymology is authoritative. But nothing is further from the truth. The scholarship of to-day, possessed by an average philologist, is far more competent to trace this or any Greek word to its real source, than Plato or Aristotle was able to do. In his analysis of Plato's Cratylus, Grote[27] observes of Plato's etymologies:—"Though sometimes reasonable enough, they are in a far greater number of instances forced, arbitrary, and fanciful. The transitions of meaning imagined, and the structural transformations of words, are alike strange and violent. Such is the light in which these Platonic etymologies appear to a modern critic. But such was not the light in which they appeared either to the ancient Platonists, or critics earlier than the last century. The Platonists even thought them full of mysterious and recondite wisdom. So complete has been the revolution of opinion that the Platonic etymologies are now treated by most critics as too absurd to

[27] Vol. II.. pp. 5:0-550.

have been seriously intended by Plato, even as conjectures. It is called 'a valuable discovery of modern times'[26] that Plato meant most of them as mere parody and caricature." The character of Aristotle as an etymologist is no better, as stated by Grote:—"Nor are they more absurd than many of the etymologies proposed by Aristotle." A slender hook this, whereon to hang such a doctrine as that of the immortal wo of countless millions of souls!

The conclusions which any judicial mind must reach from the foregoing considerations are these:—1, It is not certain from what source the word *aiōn* sprang; 2, It is of no vital consequence how it originated; 3, Aristotle's opinion is not authority; and 4, It is probable that he was not defining the word, but was alluding to that being whose *aiōn*, or existence, is continuous and eternal. That he did not understand that *aiōn* signified eternity, is evident from his uniform use of the word, in the sense of limited duration. And we find no reason in its etymology for giving it the sense of endless duration. And if it did thus originate, it does not afford a particle of proof that it was subsequently used with that meaning. It is only interesting, but never authoritative as to the meaning of a word, to ascertain its etymology. Usage is the only tribunal from which there can be no appeal.[29]

---

[26] Schleiermacher.

[29] Having read the foregoing chapter in type, Dr. White adds:—"In my etymology of αἰών, I showed that the primitive signification is 'that which goes, or moves.' In what I regard the most primitive meaning of the word in Greek, (namely, 'principle of life'), we find that the earliest meaning in Greek is really the cause of the old meaning (that which goes); this is the principle of connection between the two meanings. Again, the meaning, (3d step) 'life,' is the necessary result of the possession of the 'principle of life.' The next meaning in order ('time of a human life'), is but the natural extension of the preceding, hence 'age,' 'ages of ages,' etc., follow in natural order. Finally we see why the exact meaning of αἰών must be determined by that to which it is applied, since the time or duration of the motion of any body or thing is oftenest determined by the thing itself, e. g., the duration of motion of the heavenly bodies must be quite different from that of a bird in flight. If an adjective derives none of its meaning from the noun, what shall we say of a 'tender plant' and a 'tender heart?'"

LEXICOGRAPHY.

We now appeal to the lexicons and critics. But lexicography must be consulted concerning controverted words, *cum grano salis.* A theologian is quite certain to shade or color his definitions of technical words with his own beliefs, to lean one way or the other according to his own predilections, and tincture his definitions with his idiosyncrasies. With this thought in mind, let us consult the principal lexicographers, theologians, scholars, and Biblical critics who have explored the word. Those we shall quote comprise the most eminent of all who have testified on the subject, and present the sense which the word has been supposed to convey.

Theodoret,[1] (A. D. 300-400,) defines *aiōn* as "not any existing thing, but an interval denoting time, sometimes infinite, when spoken of God, sometimes proportioned to the duration of the creation, and sometimes to the life of man." At this early date the word certainly denoted limited duration.

Hesychius,[2] (A. D. 400-600,) defines *aiōn* thus:— "The life of man, the time of life. Euripides says life is *aiōn*." At this date no theologian had imported into the word the meaning of endless duration. It retained only the sense it had in the Classics, and in the Bible.

John of Damascus. This writer, (A. D. 750,) is one of the most eminent. Neander calls his "Accurate Expo-

---

[1] In Migne, Vol. IV., p. 40.
[2] Αἰών, ὁ βίος τῶν ἀνθρώπων, ὁ τῆς ζωῆς χρόνος .... Εὐριπίδης δὲ Φιλοκτήτῃ, Αἰῶνα τὴν ψυχὴν λέγει. Here one Greek quotes from another,— the most valuable testimony possible.

sition of the Orthodox Faith," "the most important doc-trinal text-book of the Greek church." He says:—"We should know that the word *aiōn* has many significations. For, 1. The life of every man is called *aiōn*. 2. Again, the period of 1000 years is called *aiōn*. 3. Again, the whole duration or life of this world is called *aiōn*, and, 4. The endless life after the resurrection is called the *aiōn* to come." Again:—"There are *aiōns* of *aiōns*. Since the seven *aiōns* of this present world include many *aiōns* or lives of men, and that great *aiōn* of the world includes them all, and the present *aiōn* and the *aiōn* to come is called the *aiōn* of the *aiōn*; the expressions *aiōnian* life (i. e., life of the world to come,) and *aiōnian* punishment, (i. e., punish-ment of the world to come,) disclose the endlessness of the coming *aiōn*." "Hence," says Beecher, from whom we quote,[3] "the idea of eternity is not in the word *aiōnios*, but is de-rived from the endlessness of the *aiōn* which it designates. . . . To designate the idea endless he does not here use *aiōnios*, but *aperantos*."

Zonar, a lexicographer of the eleventh century, defines *aiōn* as "a natural system of diverse bodies, embracing a logical distinction, for the sake of knowledge of God."

In the sixteenth century Phavorinus was compelled to notice an addition, which subsequently to the time of the famous Council of 544 had been grafted on the word. He says:[4]—"*Aiōn*, time, also life, also way of life. . . . . *Aiōn* is also the eternal and endless as it seems to the theo-logian." Theologians had succeeded in using the word with

---

[3] Hist. Fut. Ret., p. 292.

[4] Αἰὼν, ... ὁ χρόνος, καὶ ἡ ζωὴ, καὶ ὁ βίος. . . . Λέγεται καὶ ἀντὶ τῦ ζωῆ. Ὅμηρος, ἔπειτά με καὶ λείποι αἰὼν, ἤγουν ζωὴ. ἢ αἰὼν ζωῆ. . . . . . Ἄλλως·

Αἰὼν, ἡ ζωὴ θηλυκῶς. Ὅμηρος, Αὐτὸς δὲ φίλης αἰῶνος ἀμερθείς. παρὰ τὸ ἄειν τὸ πνέειν· καὶ ἅμα, τὸ πνεῦμα. . . . . . καὶ ἔμπνουν δὲ τὸν ζῶντα φαμέν. . . . . αἰὼν, καὶ ὁ ἀίδιος καὶ ἀτελεύτητος, ὡς τῷ Θεολόγῳ δοκεῖ·

the sense of endless, and Phavorinus was forced to recognize their usage of it, and his phraseology shows conclusively enough that he attributed to theologians the authorship of a new use of the word. Alluding to this definition, Rev. Ezra S. Goodwin, one of the ripest scholars and profoundest critics, says:[5]—"Here, I strongly suspect, is the true secret brought to light of the origin of the sense of eternity in *aiōn*. The theologian first thought he perceived it, or else he placed it there. The theologian keeps it there, now. And the theologian will probably retain it there longer than any one else. Hence it is that those lexicographers who assign eternity as one of the meanings of *aiōn* uniformly appeal for proofs to either theological, Hebrew, or Rabbinical Greek, or some species of Greek subsequent to the age of the Seventy, if not subsequent to the age of the Apostles, so far as I can ascertain." The second definition, by Phavorinus, is extracted literally from the "Etymologicon Magnum" of the ninth or tenth century. This gives us the usage from the fourth to the sixteenth century, and shows us that if the word meant endless at the time of Christ, it must have changed from limited duration in the Classics, to unlimited duration, and then back again, at the dates above specified! From the sixteenth century onward, the word has been defined as used to denote all lengths of duration from brief to endless. We record here some of the definitions we have found:

Rost, (German definitions):—"*Aiōn*, duration, epoch, long time, eternity, memory of man, life-time, life, age of man. *Aiōnios*, continual, always enduring, long continued, eternal."

Hedericus:[6]—"An age, eternity, an age as if always being; life, time of man's life, in the memory of men (wicked men— New Testament), the spinal marrow. *Aiōnios*, eternal, everlasting, continual."[7]

---

[5] Chris. Exam., Vol. X.   [6] Boston, 1833.
[7] *Ævum, æternitas; seculum, quasi ἀεὶών, vita, tempus vitæ hominis, hominum memoria, (improbi homines,* New Testament*), spinæ medulla. Aiōnios, æturnus, sempiturnus, perennis.*

Schleusner:—"Any space of time, whether longer or shorter, past, present or future, to be determined by the persons or things spoken of, and the scope of the subjects; the life or age of man. *Aiōnios*, a definite and long period of time; that is, a long enduring, but still definite period of time."

Passow:—"*Aiōnios*, long continued, eternal, everlasting, in the Classics."

Grove:[8]—"Eternity; an age, life, duration, continuance of time; a revolution of ages, a dispensation of Providence; this world or life; the world or life to come. *Aiōnios*, eternal, immortal, perpetual, former, past, ancient."

Donnegan:[9]—"Time; a space of time; life-time and life; the ordinary period of man's life; the age of man; man's estate; a long period of time; eternity; the spinal marrow. *Eis ton aiōna*, to a very long period, to eternity. *Ap aiōnos*, from or in the memory of man. *Aiōnios*, of long duration, lasting, eternal, permanent."

Ewing:—"Duration, finite or infinite; a period of duration, past or future; an age; duration of the world; ages of the world; human life in this world, or the next; our manner of life in the world; an age of divine dispensation; the ages, generally reckoned three—that before the law, that under the law, and that under the Messiah. *Aiōnios* (from preceding), ages of the world, periods of the dispensations since the world began."

Schrevelius:[10]—"An age, a long period of time; indefinite duration, time, whether longer or shorter, past, present or future; also, in the New Testament, the wicked men of the age, and also in the feminine gender, life, the life of man. *Aiōnios*, of long duration, lasting, sometimes everlasting, sometimes lasting through life, as *æturnus* in Latin."

Dr. Taylor, who wrote the Hebrew Bible three times with his own hand, says of *olam* (Greek *aiōn*), it signifies a

---

[8] Boston, 1833. [9] Phila., 1820. [10] New York, 1832.

duration which is concealed, as being of an unknown or great
length. "It signifies eternity, not from the proper force of
the word, but when the sense of the place or the nature of the
subject requires it, as God and his attributes."

Autenrieth, in his Homeric Dictionary, thus defines the
word as Homer uses it:—" αἰών, ῶνος, ὁ, (ἡ, X 58), (ἀιϜών,
aevum), *lifetime*, Δ 478, I 415; *life*, anima, T 27, X 58; with
ψυχή, Π 453, ι 523.

Pickering:—"An age, a long period of time, indefinite duration, a man's life-time, (Eurip.), life,(Æschylus),time. *Ap
aiōnos*, from or in the memory of man. *Eis ton aiōna*, for
a long time, forever, everlasting; time whether longer, or
shorter, past, present or future. Also, in New Testament, the
present age, or, men of the age, including the idea of their
corruption or depravity; the age to come, the reign of the
Messiah, the life of man, the spinal marrow. *Aiōnios*, of
long duration, lasting, sometimes everlasting, perpetual, eternal, sometimes lasting through life, as *æturnus* in Latin."

Liddell and Scott:—"A space of time, a life-time, life, also
one's time of life, age, the age of man, young in age, for one's
life long, an age, generation, one's lot in life, a long space of
time, eternity, forever; and in plural, *eis tous aiōnas tōn
aiōnōn*, unto ages of ages, forever and ever, a space of time
clearly defined and marked out, an era, age, period of a dispensation, this present life, this world, the world, the spinal
marrow."

Hincks:—"A period of time; an age, an after time, eternity. *Aiōnios*, lasting, eternal, of old, since the beginning."

Lutz:—" An age, time, eternity. *Aiōnios*, durable,
eternal."

Macknight,[11] (Scotch Presbyterian):—"These words being ambiguous, are always to be understood according to the
nature and circumstances to which they are applied." He
thinks the words sustain endless punishment, but adds:—"At
the same time I must be so candid as to acknowledge that the

---

[11] Truth of Gospel Hist., p. 28.

use of these terms, forever, eternal and everlasting, in other passages of Scripture, shows that they who understand these words in a limited sense, when applied to punishment, put no forced interpretation upon them."

Wright:—"Time, age, life-time, period, revolution of ages, dispensation of Providence, present world, or life, world to come, eternity. *Aiōnios*, eternal, ancient."

Robinson:—"Life, also, an age, that is, an indefinite long period of time, perpetuity, ever, forever, eternity, *eis ton aiōna*, ever, forever, without end, to the remotest time, forever and ever, of old, from everlasting, the world, present or future, this world and the next, present world, men of this world, world itself, advent of Messiah. *Aiōnios*, perpetual, everlasting, eternal, chiefly spoken of future time, ancient."

Jones:[12]—"An everlasting age, eternity, eternal, forever, a period of time, age, life, the present world, or life; the Jewish dispensation; a good demon, angel, as supposed to exist forever. . . *Aiōnios*, everlasting, ancient." Schweighæuser and Valpley[13] substantially agree.

Cruden:[14]—"The words eternal, everlasting, forever, are sometimes taken for a long time, and are not always to be understood strictly: for example, 'Thou shalt be our guide from this time forth, even forever,' that is, during our whole life."

Alexander Campbell:—"Its radical idea is indefinite duration."

Whitby:—"Nothing is more common and familiar in Scripture than to render a thorough and irreparable vastation, whose effects and signs should be still remaining, by the word *aiōnios*, which we render eternal." Hammond, Benson and Gilpin, in notes on Jude 7, say substantially the same.

Pearce (on Matt. 7: 33) says:—"The Greek word *aiōn* seems to signify age here, as it often does in the New Testament, and according to its most proper signification." Clarke, Giles, Wakefield, Boothroyd, Simpson, Lindsey, Mardon and

---

[12] 2d ed., London, 1825.   [13] London, ——.   [14] Concordance.

Acton, agree. So do Locke, Hammond, Le Clerc, Beausobre, Lenfant, Doddridge, Paulus, Kenrick and Olshausen."[15]

T. Southwood Smith : [16]—" Sometimes it signifies the term of human life; at other times an age, or dispensation of Providence. Its most common signification is that of age or dispensation."

Scarlett:—"That *aiōnion* does not mean endless or eternal may appear from considering that no adjective can have a greater force than the noun from which it is derived. If *aiōn* means age (which none either will or can deny), then *aiōnion* must mean age-lasting, or duration through the age or ages to which the thing spoken of relates."

Even Professor Stuart is obliged to say:[17]—The most common and appropriate meaning of *aiōn* in the New Testament, and the one which corresponds with the Hebrew word *olam*, and which, therefore, deserves the first rank in regard to order, I put down first: an indefinite period of time; time without limitation; ever, forever, time without end, eternity, all in relation to future time. The different shades by which the word is rendered, depend on the object with which *aiōn* is associated, or to which it has relation, rather than to any difference in the real meaning of the word. . . . . The question when the words are to have the meaning of absolute eternity, or when the sense of ancient, or very old, is always to be determined by the nature of the case, *i. e.*, by the context."

Maclaine: [18]—"The word *aiōn* or *aeon* is commonly used among Greek writers, but in different senses. Its signification in the Gnostic system is not very evident, and several learned men have despaired of finding out its true meaning. *Aiōn* or *aeon* among the ancients was used to signify the age

---

[15] Eternity is not given at all as a proper definition of the word by Schweighæuser, Valpley, Pickering, or Schrevelius. Age is the primary meaning, according to Schrevelius, Hedericus, Lutz and Pickering.

[16] Divine Goodness.

[17] Letters to Miller, p. 128. Exegetical Essays, sec. 4, Meaning of *Aiōn*.

[18] Maclaine's Mosheim.

of man, or the duration of human life. In after times it was employed by philosophers to express the duration of spiritual and invisible beings."

Dr. Edward Beecher[19] remarks:—"It commonly means merely continuity of action. . . . All attempts to set forth eternity as the original and primary sense of *aiōn* are at war with the facts of the Greek language for five centuries, in which it denoted life and its derivative senses, and the sense of eternity was unknown." And he also says, what is the undoubted fact, "that the original sense of *aiōn* is not eternity. . . . It is conceded on all hands that this (life) was originally the general use of the word. In the Paris edition of Henry Stephens' Lexicon it is affirmed emphatically 'that life, or the space of life, is the primitive sense of the word, and that it is always so used by Homer, Hesiod, and the old poets; also by Pindar and the tragic writers, as well as by Herodotus and Xenophon.' 'Pertaining to the world to come,' is the sense given to 'These shall go away into everlasting punishment,' by Prof. Tayler Lewis, who adds,[20]—'The preacher in contending with the Universalist and the Restorationist, would commit an error, and it may be suffer a failure in his argument, should he lay the whole stress of it on the etymological or historical significance of the words *aiōn*, *aiōnios*, and attempt to prove that of themselves they necessarily carry the meaning of endless duration. 'These shall go away into the restraint, imprisonment of the world to come,' is all we can etymologically or exegetically make of the word in this passage.'"

Undoubtedly the definition given by Schleusner is the accurate one,—"Duration determined by the subject to which it is applied." Thus it only expresses the idea of endlessness when connected with what is eternal, as God. The word great is an illustrative word. Great applied to a tree, or mountain, or man, denotes a different degree in each case, but when refer-

---

[19] Hist. Fut. Ret.
[20] Lange's Ecclesiastes.

ring to God, it has the sense of infinite. Infinity does not reside
in the word great, but it has that meaning when applied to
God. It does not impart it to God; it derives it from him.
So of *aiōnion;* applied to Jonah's residence in the fish, it
means seventy hours; to the priesthood of Aaron, it signifies
several centuries; to the mountains, thousands of years; to
the punishments of a merciful God, as long as is necessary to
vindicate his law and reform his children; to God himself,
eternity. What great is to size, *aiōnios* is to duration. Human beings live from a few hours to a century; nations from
a century to thousands of years; and worlds, for aught we
know, from a few to many millions of years; and God is eternal. So that when we see the word applied to a human life it
denotes somewhere from a few days to a hundred years; when
it is applied to a nation, it denotes anywhere from a century
to ten thousand years, more or less, and when to God it means
endless. In other words, it practically denotes indefinite duration, as we shall see when we meet the word in sacred and
secular literature. Dr. Beecher well observes:[21]—"There are
six ages, or aggregates of ages, involving temporary systems,
spoken of in the Old Testament. These ages are distinctly
stated to be temporary, and yet to them all are applied *olam*
and its reduplications, as fully and emphatically as they are to
God. This is a positive demonstration that the word *olam,*
or *aiōn,* as affirmed by Taylor and Fürst in their Hebrew
Concordances, means an indefinite period or age, past or
future, and not an absolute eternity. When applied to God,
the idea of eternity is derived from him and not from the
word. . . . This indefinite division of time is represented
by *olam* (Greek *aiōn*). Hence we find, since there are many
ages, or periods, that the word is used in the plural. Moreover, since one great period or age can comprehend under it
subordinate ages, we find such expressions as an age of ages,
or an *olam* of *olams,* and other reduplications. In some
cases, however, the reduplication of *olam* seems to be a rhetor-

---

[21] Hist. Fut. Ret.

ical amplification of the idea, without any comprehension of ages by a greater age. This is especially true when *olam* is in the singular in both parts of the reduplication, as 'to the age of the age.' The use of the word in the plural is decisive evidence that the sense of the word is not eternity, in the absolute sense, for there can be but one such eternity. But as time past and future can be divided by ages, so there may be many ages, and an age of ages."

John Foster, the celebrated Baptist, declares:[22]—"I hope it is not presumptuous to take advantage of the fact that the terms everlasting, eternal, forever, original or translated, are often employed in the Bible, as well as other writings, under great and various limitations of import; and are thus withdrawn from the predicament of necessarily and absolutely meaning a strictly endless duration. The limitation is often, indeed, plainly marked by the nature of the subject. In other instances the words are used with a figurative indefiniteness, which leaves the limitation to be made by some general rule of reason and proportion. They are designed to magnify, to aggravate, rather than to define. . . . . . I therefore conclude that a limited interpretation is authorized."

Simpson, in his Essays, says:[23]—"*Æon* occurs about a hundred times in the New Testament, [in all, one hundred and twenty-eight times,] in seventy of which, at least, it is clearly used for a limited duration. In the Septuagint translation of the Old Testament it is even repeated, and several times it is repeated twice, without meaning eternity; and in two instances it signifies no longer a period than the life of one man only. It is an observation of the utmost importance, that when αἰών, or αἰώνιος, is applied to the future punishment of the wicked, they are never joined to life, immortality, incorruptibility, but are always connected with fire, or with that punishment, pain, destruction, or second death, which is effected by means of fire. Now, since fire, which consumes

---

[22] Life and Cor. Letter to a Young Minister.
[23] Quoted by T. Southwood Smith, in Divine Goodness.

or decomposes other perishable bodies, is of itself of a dis-
soluble or perishing nature, this intimates a limitation of the
period of time."

It will be of interest to give here the views of Thomas De
Quincey, one of the most accurate students of language, and
profoundest reasoners and thinkers among English scholars,
as well as one of the best Greek scholars:[24]—"I used to be
annoyed and irritated by the false interpretation given to the
Greek word *aiōn*, and given necessarily, therefore, to the
Greek adjective *aiōnios* as its immediate derivative. It was
not so much the falsehood of this interpretation, as the nar-
rowness of that falsehood that disturbed me. . . . . The
reason which gives to this word *aiōnion* what I do not scruple
to call a dreadful importance, is the same reason, and no other,
which prompted the dishonesty concerned in the ordinary interpretation of this word. The word happened to connect
itself—but that was no practical concern of mine,—me it had
not biased in the one direction, nor should it have biased any
just critic in the counter direction—happened, I say, to connect itself with the ancient dispute upon the duration of
future punishment. What was meant by the *aiōnion* punishments of the next world? Was the proper sense of the
word eternal, or was it not? . . . . That argument runs
thus—that the ordinary construction of the word *aiōnion*, as
equivalent to everlasting, could not possibly be given up, when
associated with penal misery, because in that case, and by the
very same act, the idea of eternity must be abandoned as
applicable to the counter bliss of paradise. Torment and
blessedness, it was argued, punishment and beatification, stood
upon the same level; the same word it was, the word *aiōnion*,
which qualified the duration of either; and if eternity, in the
most rigorous acceptation, fell away from the one idea, it must
equally fall away from the other. Well, be it so. But that
would not settle the question. It might be very painful to
renounce a long-cherished anticipation, but the necessity of

---

[24] Theological Essays.

doing so could not be received as a sufficient reason for adhering to the old unconditional use of the word *aiōnion*. The argument is, that we must retain the old sense of eternal, because else we lose upon one scale what we have gained upon the other. But what then? would be the reasonable man's retort. We are not to accept or reject a new construction (if otherwise the more colorable) of the word *aiōnion*, simply because the consequences might seem such, as, upon the whole, to displease us. We may gain nothing; for by the new interpretation our loss may balance our gain, and we may prefer the old arrangement. But how monstrous is all this! We are not summoned as to a choice of two different arrangements that may suit different tastes, but to a grave question as to what is the sense and operation of the word *aiōnion*.

.   .   Meantime, all this speculation, first and last, is pure nonsense. *Aiōnian* does not mean eternal, neither does it mean of limited duration. Nor would the unsettling of *aiōnian* in its old use, as applied to punishment, to torment, to misery, etc., carry with it any necessary unsettling of the idea in its application to the beatitudes of Paradise.

"What is an *aiōn*? The duration or cycle of existence which belongs to any object, not individually of itself, but universally, in right of its genius.   .   ˙   .   Man has a certain *aiōnian* life; possibly ranging somewhere about the period of seventy years assigned in the Psalms.   .   .

.   .   The period would in that case represent the '*aiōn*' of the individual Tellurian; but the *aiōn* of the Tellurian race would probably amount to many millions of our earthly years, and it would remain an unfathomable mystery, deriving no light at all from the septuagenarian '*aiōn*' of the individual; though between the two *aiōns* I have no doubt that some secret link of connection does and must subsist, however undiscoverable by human sagacity.

"This only is discoverable, as a general tendency, that the *aiōn*, or generic period of evil is constantly towards a fugitive duration. The *aiōn*, it is alleged, must always express the same idea, whatever that may be; if it is less than eternity for the evil cases, then it must be less for the good ones. Doubtless the idea of an *aiōn* is in one sense always uniform, always the same,—viz., as a tenth or a twelfth is always the same. Arithmetic could not exist if any caprice or variation affected their ideas—a tenth is always more than an eleventh, always less than a ninth. But this uniformity of ratio and proportion does not hinder but that a tenth may now represent a guinea, and the next moment represent a thousand guineas. The exact amount of the duration expressed by an *aiōn* depends altogether upon the particular subject which yields the *aiōn*. It is, as I have said, a radix, and like an algebraic square-foot or cube-foot, though governed by the most rigorous laws of limitation, it must vary in obedience to the nature of the particular subject whose radix it forms." De Quincey's conclusions are:

"A. That man who allows himself to infer the eternity of evil from the counter eternity of good, builds upon the mistake of assigning a stationary and mechanic value to the idea of an *aiōn*, whereas the very purpose of Scripture in using the word was to evade such a value. The word is always varying for the very purpose of keeping it faithful to a spiritual identity. The period or duration of every object would be an essentially variable quantity, were it not mysteriously commensurate to the inner nature of that object as laid open to the eyes of God. And thus it happens that everything in the world, possibly without a solitary exception, has its own separate *aiōn*; how many entities, so many *aiōns*.

"B. But if it be an excess of blindness which can overlook the *aiōnian* differences amongst even neutral entities, much deeper is that blindness which overlooks the separate tendencies of things evil and things good. Naturally, all evil is fugitive and allied to death.

"C. I, separately, speaking for myself only, profoundly believe that the Scriptures ascribe absolute and metaphysical eternity to one sole being,—viz., God; and derivatively to all others according to the interest which they can plead in God's favor. Having anchorage in God, innumerable entities may possibly be admitted to a participation in divine *aiōn*. But what interest in the favor of God can belong to falsehood, to malignity, to impurity? To invest them with *aiōnian* privileges, is, in effect, and by its results, to distrust and to insult the Deity. Evil would not be evil, if it had that power of self-subsistence which is imparted to it in supposing its *aiōnian* life to be co-eternal with that which crowns and glorifies the good."

Says Rev. Edmund H. Sears:[25]—"The word *aiōn* and its derivatives, rendered 'eternal' and 'everlasting,' describe an economy complete in itself, and the duration must depend on the nature of the economy. . . . The New Testament, if it reveals anything, reveals the *aiōn*—the dispensation that lies next to this, and gathers into it the momentous results of our probation in time. But what lies beyond that in the cycles of a coming eternity, I do not believe has been revealed to the highest angel. Think of that endless Beyond! If every atom of the globe were counted off, and every atom stood for a million years, still we have not approached a conception of endless duration. And yet sinful and fallible men affirm that their fellow sinners are to be given over to indescribable agonies through those millions of years thus repeated, and even then the clocks of eternity have only struck the morning hour! that the hells of pent-up anguish are to streak eternity with blood in lines parallel forever with the being of God. If Gabriel should come and tell us that, we should have a right to believe that the history of the infinite future infolded in the bosom of God, had not been given to Gabriel."

Dr. Pusey, a strenuous defender of endless hell torments, admits,[26] that the word only means "endless within the sphere of its own existence."

It does not seem to have been generally considered by students of this subject that the thought of endless duration

---

[25] Sermons, pp. 99-102.
[26] Canon Farrar, Excursus on the word *aiōnios*, in Eternal Hope.

is comparatively a modern conception.[27] The ancients, at a time more recent than the date of the Old Testament, had not yet cognized the idea of endless duration, so that passages containing the word applied to God do not mean that he is of eternal duration, but the idea in their minds was of indefinite duration.

De Lamennais:[28]—"In Hebrew and Greek the words rendered everlasting have not this sense. They signify 'a duration of time,' a period, whence the phrase, 'during these eternities and beyond.' "

De Wette says :[29]—"The doctrine of eternal damnation cannot in any wise be retained, if we take the word eternal in a strict and absolute sense. For whatever is eternally damned, must have been created in a state of eternal damnation; for eternity has no beginning."

Professor Blackie, Greek professor in the university of Edinburgh, observes[30]:—"It doesn't require any very profound scholarship to know that the word aiōnios, which we translate everlasting, does not signify eternity, absolutely and metaphysically, but only popularly, as when we say that a man is an eternal fool, meaning by that he is a very great fool."

Canon Farrar's testimony is equally positive:[31]—"Now, I ask you, my brethren, very solemnly, where would be the popular teachings about hell if we calmly and deliberately erased from our English Bible the three words, 'damnation,' 'hell,' and 'everlasting'? Yet I say, unhesitatingly,—I say, claiming the fullest right to speak with the authority of knowledge—I say, with the calmest and most unflinching sense of responsibility—I say, standing here in the sight of God and of my Savior, and, it may be, of the angels and spirits of the dead, that not one of those words ought to stand any longer in the English Bible, and that being, in our

[27] Pp. 11, 12, of this volume.
[28] Canon Farrar, Excursus V., Eternal Hope.
[29] Theol. Zeitschrift, Vol. II.
[30] Nat. Hist. Atheism, p. 201.   [31] Eternal Hope.

present acceptation of them, simply mistranslations, they most unquestionably will not stand in the revised version of the Bible, if the revisers have understood their duty. The word '*aiōnios*,' translated 'everlasting,' is simply the word which, in its first sense, means 'age-long' or '*eoneon*,' and it is, in the Bible itself, applied over and over again to things which have utterly and long since passed away; and in its second sense, it is something above and beyond time—something spiritual, as when the knowledge of God is said to have eternal or '*eoneon*' life. So that when, with your futile billions of years, you foist into the word '*aiōnios*' the fiction of an endless time, you do but give the lie to the mighty oath of that great angel who set one foot on the sea and the other on the land, and with one hand uplifted to heaven, sware by him that liveth forever, that time should be no more. . . There is no authority whatever for rendering it everlasting."

The Emphatic Diaglott :[32]—"Age, *aioon*, an indefinite period of time, past, present or future. This is the proper translation of *aioon*, which in the common version is often improperly rendered *world*, *always*, and *forever*. The word occurs about 100 times in its singular and plural forms. The adjective form of the same word, *aioonios*, is found about 75 times, and is applied to *zoe*, *life*, 45 times, to *fire* 3 times, to *glory* 3 times, etc. *Eternal* or *everlasting*, as generally understood, is an improper translation of *aioonios*; in fact, we have no proper equivalent in the English language. Being an adjective, and derived from the noun *aioon*, *age*, it cannot properly go beyond its meaning." [33]

---

[32] New York, S. R. Wells.

[33] Hesychius, as we have shown, says it is sometimes used for "a long time;" and Origen alludes to the same fact. In Exod. Hom. vi : 13 ; ii : 3, 5. Leontius Byzantinus, even in arguing against Origenists, admits that both in profane and sacred literature *aiōn* is used as a definite period. Cæsarius (Dial. 3) even observes that the Origenist argument on the terminability of torment was derived from the use of this very word. Huetius, Origeniana (Op. ed. Paris, iv : pp. 231, 233).

Charles Kingsley, of the English Church, the celebrated author, wrote in a letter not long before his death [34]:—"That the true meanings of the word *aiōn* and *aiōnios* have little or nothing to do with it, even if *aiōn* be derived from *aei*, always, which I greatly doubt. The word never is used in Scripture anywhere else in the sense of endlessness (vulgarly called eternity). It always meant, both in Scripture and out, a period of time. Else how could it have a plural?—how could you talk of the *aiōns* and *aeons* of *aeons*, as the Scripture does? Nay, more, how talk of *outos aiōn*, which the translators, with laudable inconsistency, have translated— this world, *i. e.*, this present state of things, age, dispensation—epoch. *Aiōnios*, therefore, means, and must mean, belonging to an epoch, and *aiōnios kolasis* is the punishment belonging to that epoch. Always bear in mind, what Maurice insists on,—and what is so plain to honest readers,— that our Lord and the Apostles always speak of being in the end of an age or *aeon*, not as ushering in a new one, coming to judge and punish the old world; and to create a new one out of its ruins, or rather, as the Sunday-school better expresses it, to burn up the chaff and keep the wheat, *i. e.*, all the elements of food, as seed for the new world."

Certainly the aggregate of these testimonies, from those who have made the word a careful study, compels us to deny to it the sense of endless duration, and disposes us to understand it as denoting limited duration, unless the connection in which it is found necessitates a different sense.

We pause here and raise this question:—Is it possible that our Heavenly Father had created a world of endless torture, to which his children for thousands of years were crowding in myriads, and that he not only had not revealed the fact to them, but was so short-sighted that he had not given them a word to express the fact, or even a capacity sufficient to bring the idea of the eternal suffering to which they were liable within

---

[34] Life and Letters.

the compass of their cognition? He created the horse for man's use, and created man capable of comprehending the horse; he surrounded him with multitudes of animate and inanimate objects, each of which he could name and comprehend, but the most important reality of all—one which must be believed in, or eternal woe is the penalty, man not only had no name for, but he was incapable of the faintest conception of the mere fact! Would, or could a good Father be guilty of such an omission?

Can anything be clearer than this—that the critics unite in saying that limited duration is not only allowable, but that it is the prevailing signification of the word? Do they not agree that eternal duration is not in the word, and can only be imported into it by the subject associated with it?

Thus, limited duration is the force of the word,—duration to be determined by the subject treated, if we allow Etymology and Lexicography to declare the verdict; and every reader of the Bible ought to enter upon its reading—after having studied the etymology and lexicography of the word—prejudiced in favor of giving to it, wherever found, the meaning of limited duration.

In tracing the usage of the word, our sources of information will be (1) The Greek Classics, (2) The Septuagint, (3) Jewish Greeks contemporary with Christ, (4) The New Testament, (5) Early Christian Writers.

It is a vital question, How was the word used in the Greek literature with which the Seventy were familiar,—that is, the Greek Classics?

When the Old Testament was translated from Hebrew into Greek, by the Seventy, the word had been in common use for many centuries. It is preposterous to say that the Seventy would render the Hebrew by the Greek, and give to the latter a different meaning from that of the former, or a different meaning from *aiōn* in current Greek literature. It is self-evident that *aiōn* in the Old Testament must mean exactly what *olam* means, and also what *aiōn* means in the Greek Classics. Indefinite duration is the sense of *olam*, and it is perfectly clear that *aiōn* must have the same signification. As we examine the word in the Classics we find that it was generally used in a sense from which eternal duration is absolutely excluded.

The oldest author is Homer, 1,000 B. C. In his Iliad and Odyssey *aiōn* occurs thirteen[1] times as a noun, always.

---

[1] We give here the thirteen instances :—Iliad, XXII: 58, Αὐτὸς δὲ φίλης αἰῶνος ἀπερθῆς Il., XXIV: 725, 'Ανερ, ἀπ' αἰῶνος νέος ὤλεο. Il., IV: 478: XVII: 302, Μινυνθάδιος . . . αἰών, A briefly durable life. Il., IX; 415, 'Επὶ δηρὸν δέ μοι αἰὼν ἔσσεται, My life shall be for a long period. Il., V: 685, 'Επειτά με καὶ λίποι αἰὼν ἐν πόλει ὑμετέρῃ," Let life forsake me in your city. Il., XVI: 453, 'Επὴν δὴ τόνγε λίπῃ ψυχή τε καὶ αἰών· Juno advises Jupiter to suffer Sarpedon to die, and to have him buried after *life*, and his soul have left him. Il., XIX: 27, 'Εκ δ' αἰὼν πέφαται· κατὰ δὲ χρόα πάντα σαπήῃ, The life has been expelled. In the Odyssey, V: 152, Κατείβετο δὲ γλυκὺς αἰών, νόστον ὀδυρομένῳ, His (Ulysses') sweet *life* was exhaling because anxious to return home. Od., V: 160, Μηδέ τοι αἰὼν φθινέτω,

Not in a single instance, as found in the oldest of Greek poets, Homer, is the word used to express the idea of eternal duration. Priam to Hector says,[2] "Thou shalt be deprived of pleasant *aiōnos*" (life). Andromache over dead Hector,[3] "Husband, thou hast perished from *aiōnos*" (life or time). The other instances have the same meaning. Dr. Beecher writes:[4]—"But there is a case that excludes all possibility of doubt or evasion, in the Homeric Hymn of Mercury, vs. 42 and 119. Here *aiōn* is used to denote the marrow, as the life of an animal, as Moses calls the blood the life. This is recognized by Crusius in his Homeric Lexicon. In this case to pierce the life (*aiōn*) of a turtle means to pierce the spinal cord. The idea of life is here exclusive of time or eternity." These are fair illustrations of Homer's use of the word.

Hesiod (800 B. C.), employs it twice:[5]—"To him (the married man) during *aiōnos* (life) evil is constantly striving, etc."

Æschylus (525 B. C.), has the word twenty-one times, after this manner:—"This life (*aiōn*) seems long," etc.[6] "Jupiter, king of the never-ceasing world"[7] (*aiōnos apaustou*).

Pindar (522 B. C.) gives eighteen instances, such as[8] "A long life produces the four virtues."

Sophocles (B. C. 495), uses *aiōn* nine times, *makraiōn*

Nor let your *life* escape. Od., VII: 224, Ἰδόντα με καὶ λίποι αἰὼν κτῆσιν ἐμὴν δμωάς τε, καὶ ὑψερεφὲς μέγα δῶμα, Let *life* forsake me, etc. Od., IX: 523, Ψυχῆς τε καὶ αἰῶνος . . . εὖνιν ποιήσας Having deprived you of *life* and soul. Od., XVIII: 204, Ὀδυρομένη κατὰ θυμὸν αἰῶνα φθινύθω. Penelope here asks Diana to let her die ; that grief may no longer consume her *life*.

[2] Il., XXII : 58.   [3] Il., XXIV : 725.   [4] Hist. Fut. Ret.

[5] Theog., 609, Τῷ δὲ ἀπ' αἰῶνος κακὸν ἐσθλῷ ἀντιφέριζει ἔμμεναι. Also Scut. Herc., 331.

[6] Persæ, 263.

[7] Supp., 570. Cited by Tayler Lewis. It also occurs, Prom. 860 ; Sept. Con. Theb., 219 ; ib., 744 ; ib., 774 ; Suppl., 47 ; ib., 577 ; Agam., 107 ; ib., 230 ; ib., 249 ; ib., 556 ; ib., 716 ; ib., 1150 ; Choeph., 24 ; ib., 348 ; ib., 440 ; Eumen., 315 ; ib., 560 ; Pers., 1007 ; Prom. 107.

[8] Nem., III : 130. The passages in Pindar found in his Odes are, Olymp., II : 18, 121 ; IX : 90 ; Pyth., III : 153 ; IV : 331 ; V : 8 ; VIII : 139 ; Nem., II : 11 ; III : 130 ; IX ; 106 ; Isthm., III : 29 ; VII : 59 ; VIII : 27 ; Fragments (Donaldson's ed.) lxxvii : 3 ; xcii : 2 ; xcvi : 3 ; cxlvi.

4

five times, *euaiōn* three times.[9] Long is employed by him to increase the force of *aiōn*, which would be worse than superfluous if the word of itself signified interminable duration.

Hippocrates (460 B. C.):· "A human *aiōn* is a seven days' matter."[10]

Euripides (480 B. C.), uses the word thirty-two times. We quote four instances:—[11] "Marriage to those mortals who are well situated is a happy *aiōn*."[12] "Every *aiōn* of mortals

---

[9] Elect. 1030:—Ἄσκει τοιαίτη νοῦν δι' αἰῶνος μένειν, Try to continue the same in mind during life. Ib., 1091, Καὶ σὺ πάγκλαυτον αἰῶνα κοινὸν εἵλου, —And thou has constantly chosen a sorrowful life. Ajax Flag., 657,

'Ω τλάμων πάτερ,
Οἵαν σε μένει πυθέσθαι
Παιδὸς δύσφορον ἄταν,
'Αν οὔπω τις ἔθρεψεν
Αἰὼν Αἰακιδᾶν
'Ατερθέ γε τοῦδε.

—Unhappy father, what a sad calamity you are soon to learn concerning your son, such as no one, (that is, who ever lived, no life,) ever endured in the family of Æacus, but this one. Antig. 589, Εὐδαίμονες, οἷσι κακῶν ἀγευστος αἰών.—Whose *life* is free from a taste of evils. Œdip. Colon., 1812. Ποῖ δῆτ' αὖθις ὧδ' ἔρημος, ἄπορος, αἰῶνα τλάμων ἔξω,—Where shall I support life, desolate and overwhelmed hereafter? Trachiniæ, 2, Οὐκ ἂν αἰὼν ἐκμάθοι βροτῶν, πρὶν ἂν θάνοι τις, οὔτ' εἰ χρηστὸς, οὔτ' εἰ τῷ κακός,—No one can know the *life* of mortals before he has died, whether good or evil to any. Ibid., 34, Τοιοῦτος αἰὼν εἰς δόμους τε κὰκ δόμων αἰεὶ τὸν ἄνδρ' ἔπεμπε λατρεύοντα τῳ.—Such a life, at home and abroad, is always awaiting the man who is a servant to any one. Philoc. 179, 'Ω δίστανα γένη βροτῶν, οἷς μὴ μέτριος αἰών,—O miserable race of mortals, who have not a *life* of mediocrity. Ib. 1390, 'Ω στιγνὸς αἰὼν, τί μ' ἔτι δῆτ' ἔχεις ἄνω βλέποντα, κοὐκ ἀφῆκας εἰς ᾅδου μολεῖν,—Ah, detestable life, why still detain me here above, and not permit me to depart to the grave? He also uses μακραίων five times,(Œd. Tyr. 526, 1118; Ajax Flag. 195; Antigone, 999; Œd. Col. 148, 9) in the sense of long life and εὐαίων as happy life three times, (Trach. 81; Philoc. 855). No other meaning than we have ascribed is possible.

[10] *Peri Sarkōn.* Hippocrates says:—The human *aiōn* is so clearly only a seven-days' matter that if it will but refrain from eating and drinking seven days it will die. He uses the word just as Aristotle does.

[11] Orestes, 596.   [12] Ibid, 971.

is unstable." [13] "A long *aiōn* has many things to say," etc. [14] "He breathed out the *aiōna*."

Empedocles, (444 B. C.):—"An earthly body deprived of happy life," (*aiōnos*).[15]

Isocrates, (436 B. C.):[16]—"Those who live with piety and righteousness, both continue securely in the present time, and concerning the whole *aiōn* have their hopes very sweet." Of those who understand the Eleusinian mysteries, he says:— They "have very sweet hopes concerning the end of life, and the whole *aiōn*." Evidently life is here the exact equivalent of *aiōn*.

Professor Clarke quotes many passages from later writers, such as Erinna (560 B. C.), Euripides (450 B. C.), Epictetus (140 A. D.), Plutarch (160 A. D.), Diodorus (75 B. C.), Alcinous, Philo Judaeus (A. D., 60), and others, and inclines to the view that they gave the meaning of eternity to the word, and that the adjective always means endless; but a careful reading of his citations satisfies us that the passages employ the word in the sense of life—Greek *bios*—the duration of it to be determined by the connections. We give a few of his quotations:—"Diodorus, in the first century before Christ, wrote, 'Joining the order of the stars and the natures of men into a common analogy, it circles continuously through all the *aiōn*.' Again he says, 'Some, presuming that the cosmos is unborn and imperishable, have affirmed that the race of men has existed from *aiōn*.' Again, 'By fear of harm of their bodies, and of disgraced repute for all the *aiōn*'—(referring to deprivation of

---

[13] Med., 428. The other passages are found in Hec., 754; Phœniss. 1498; Med. 248, 646; Androm, 1218; Suppl., 1008; Iphigen. in Aul., 1517; Iphigen. in Taur., 1129; Bacch., 92; Suppl., 962 (in comp.); Bacch., 426; Phœniss., 1537; Hippol., 1444; Alcest., 486; Bacch., 395; Heracl., 903; Ion, 637; Phœniss., 1549; Suppl., 962, 1087; Helen, 215; Ion, 126; Herc. Fur. 673; Iphigen. in Aul., 552. ——. Suppl. 962; Bacch. 426; Ion 126; and Iph. Aul. 552 are the compound adjective.

[14] Philoc., quoted by Hesychius.

[15] Quoted by Hierocles.

[16] Quoted by Prof. J. C. C. Clarke, Professor of Greek in Shurtleff College, Illinois.

religious burial supposed necessary for souls). Again he writes,
'To spend the *aiōn* in the approaching Hades with the pious.'
About the Christian era, and for several centuries later,
there were hosts in all Greek-speaking nations who believed
that there had emanated from God, before time began, a number of lesser deities who would live forever. These they called
aiōnes, imitating Plato imperfectly, or following a still older
idea. For Erinna, a poetess early in the sixth century
before Christ, in an ode to the goddess Rhome (Might) wrote,
'To thee alone, the greatest Aion, who shakes all things, and
transforms life variously, does not change the favoring wind
of rule.' And Euripides, in the fifth century, wrote, ' Many
things does Fate produce, and Aion, Son of Kronos.' In the
second century after Christ, Epictetus wrote, 'I am not an
aiōn, but a man.' Plutarch, in the second century, said of sui-
cides, ' They must not thus go to *aiōn*.' "

Dr. Beecher gives these and other instances, most or all
of which we believe we have cited. Andromache over Hector,
(Il. XXIV, 725), "Too early hast thou perished from life," (*aiōn*). Sarpedon to Hector, "Do not permit my life (*aiōn*) to
leave me." In Hymn to Mercury (vs. 42, 119), the god is described as destroying the life (*aiōn*) of a mountain tortoise,
and the lives (*aiōnas*) of two cows to prepare a feast. In
Pindar (Hypochor. III., 5), "His life (*aiōn*) was dashed out
through his bones." Æschylus says (Prometheus, 862), "Each
wife shall deprive her husband of life" (*aiōn*). Euripides
(Orestes, 603), "a happy life" (*aiōn*). In Bacchae Semele "left
this life" (*aiōn*). Sophocles, (Philoctetes, 179,) "O! miserable
generations of mortals, to whom not even a tolerable life (*aiōn*)
is assigned." Also (1348) "O! sad, hateful, gloomy life" (*aiōn*).
Euripedes, (Hecuba, 754-7,) Agamemnon to Hecuba, "Your ser-
vile life" (*aiōn*). Hecuba replies, "To be in servitude all my
life" (*aiōn*). He insists that endless duration is not contained
in the word.

Rev. Ezra S. Goodwin [17] has patiently and candidly traced

---

[17] Chris. Exam., Vols. X, XI, and XIII.

this word through the Classics, finding the noun frequently in nearly all the writers, but not meeting the adjective until Plato, its inventor, used it. He states, as the result of his protracted and exhaustive examination from the beginning down to Plato, "We have the whole evidence of seven Greek writers, extending through about six centuries, down to the age of Plato, who make use of *aiōn* in common with other words, and *no one of them* EVER employs *it in the sense of eternity.*"

Plato (429 B. C.) employs the noun as his predecessors had done, "Leading a life (*aiōna*) involved in troubles."[18] He uses *aiōn* eight times, *aiōnios* five, *diaiōnios* once, and *makraiōn*, twice. If he regarded the noun as signifying eternity he would not attach prefixes signifying short and long.

Prof. Clarke[19] quotes from Plato's Timæus. Plato had said that God, in making the visible heaven out of eternal essence, imitated the best divine essence he could see, and the duration of it is an *aiōn*. Plato then says, according to Prof. Clarke, "The pattern was an infinite or eternal living being —a real being through all eternity" (*aiōn*). But why not say duration, or being, instead of "eternity"? Is not the meaning here equivalent to that of the Greek *bios*?

Plato employs four instances of *aiōn*, three of *aiōnios*, and one of *diaiōnios* in a single passage,[20] in contrast with *aïdios* (eternal). The gods he calls eternal (*aïdios*), but the soul and the corporeal nature are *aiōnios*, belonging to time, and "all these," "are part of time." And he calls time (*Kronos*) an *aiōnios* image of *Aiōnos*. Exactly what so obscure an author may mean here is not apparent, but one thing is perfectly clear, he cannot mean eternity and eternal by *aiōnos* and *aiōnion*, for nothing is wider from the fact than that fluctuating, changing time, beginning and ending, and full of

---

[18] De Leg. Lib. III. These are the passages in which Plato employs the words:—Protag., Vol. I; Gorgias, De Leg., Lib. X; Axioch. Vol. III; Timæus; De Repub., Lib. II; De Leg., Lib. X, and Phædon.

[19] "Is Aionion Endless?" articles in New York Examiner and Chronicle.

[20] Timæus.

mutations, is an image of eternity. It is in every possible particular its exact opposite.[21]

The adjective *aiōnios* is found in none of the authors above quoted, except Plato. Mr. Goodwin thinks that Plato coined it, for even Socrates, the teacher of Plato, does not use it. In all the Greek literature covering a period of more than six hundred years, the word is never found. Of course it must mean the same as the noun that is its source. It having clearly appeared that the noun is uniformly used to denote limited duration, and never to signify eternity, it is equally apparent that the adjective must mean the same. The noun sweetness gives its flavor to its adjective, sweet. The adjective long means precisely the same as the noun length. When sweet stands for acidity, and long represents brevity, *aiōnios* can properly mean eternal, derived from *aiōn*, limited duration. To say that Plato, the inventor of the word, has used the adjective to mean eternal, when neither he nor any of his predecessors ever used the noun to denote eternity, would be to charge one of the wisest of men with etymological stupidity. Has he been guilty of such folly? How does he use the word? Referring to certain souls in Hades,[22] he describes them as in *aiōnion* intoxication. But that he does not use the word in the sense of endless is evident from the Phædon, where he says, "It is a very ancient opinion that souls quitting this world repair to the infernal regions, and *return after that, to live in this world.*" After the *aiōnion* intoxication is over, they return to earth, which

---

[21] See Protag., Vol. I.:—My lot in life (μοῖραν αἰῶνος). Gorg.,—life, being, (τὸν αἰῶνα ἡμῶν). De Leg., Lib. III:—a wretched life (χαλεπὸν αἰῶνα). Axiochus, Vol. III. What the author meant here is not clear. He could not have meant eternity. He says:—"If human nature could have seen that the relations of this world are associated (εἰς τὸν αἰῶνα) in an organization, into life, a complete entity or being." The meaning is obscure except that eternity is not possible. *Makraiōn* occurs in De Repub. Lib. II, and Epin. Vol. II (probably by one of Plato's disciples). The "ancient opinion" he quotes from Musæus.

[22] De Repub., Lib. II.

demonstrates that the word was not used by him as meaning endless. Again,[23] he speaks of that which is indestructible, (*anolethron*) and not *aiōnion*. He places the two words in contrast, whereas, had he intended to use *aiōnion* to mean endless, he would have said indestructible *and aiōnion*.

The adjective occurs in Plato five times.[24] "The best recompense of virtue is continual elevation," or "constant exaltation,"—literally, "life-long intoxication," μέθην αἰώνιον. He calls the soul and body indestructible and not *aiōnion*.[25] Temporal duration is the meaning here, for *aiōnion* is contrasted with indestructible. In the Timæus *aiōnios* occurs three times. The gods, he says, are ἀίδιον, eternal, but the animal is αἰώνιον, as God created an *aiōnian* image of being, which we name time. Time and the heavens were generated together, so that if there should ever be a dissolution of them, they might be as much alike as possible; they both have an *aiōnian* nature. He then adds that the stars are made like a living being, with an imitation of an *aiōnian* nature, πρὸς τὴν τῆς διαιωνίας μίμησιν φύσεως. It is not easy to put Plato's meaning into plain English, but nothing can be clearer than that these first five recorded instances of the occurrence of the adjective do not signify endless duration.

Plato has been supposed by many to teach the eternity of the torments of the wicked. But if anything is clearly taught by him, it is that the various transmigrations of all souls will result at length in their purification.[26] He most distinctly teaches that punishment will end in the advantage of the punished.[27] His use of the word discussed in this monograph in connection with punishment is not, as has been so often supposed, a proof of his belief in that doctrine, because, as

23 De Leg., Lib. X.
24 De Repub., Lib. II.
25 Ibid:—ἀνώλεθρον δὲ ὂν γενόμενον, ἀλλ᾽ οὐκ αἰώνιον, ψυχὴν καὶ σῶμα.
26 This is in the Timæus, Gorgias and Phædon very plainly set forth.
27 De Repub.

Olympiodorus shows,[23] Plato applied the word to the heavenly spheres, meaning a cycle or *œōn*, throughout which some souls would be punished. Olympiodorus well observes:—"Punishment cannot be eternal. An unending pain can do no good, for it is useless. God and nature do nothing in vain." Plato's use of the word was in entire harmony with its meaning throughout the Classics.

We cite passages from Aristotle: De Mundo, Cap. 2:— "The stars move harmoniously during their existence"(δι' αἰῶνος). Ibid, Cap. 5:—"The stars and moon move from one epoch, or *œōn*, to another,"(ἐξ αἰῶνος εἰς ἕτερον αἰῶνα). Ib.:—Of the earth's changes, he says they are for her safety during her life, (τὴν δι' αἰῶνος σωτηρίαν παρέχειν). Ib.:—The existence or being of earth is described:—φυλάττει τὸ σίμπαν ἄφθαρτον δι' αἰῶνος. Cap. 7:— "God's existence extends from one age, or *œōn*, to another," (διήκων ἐξ αἰῶνος ἀτέρμονος εἰς ἕτερον αἰῶνα). Metaph. Lib. XIV., Cap. 7:—"Life and a *being* perpetual and eternal belong to God," (ὥστε ζωὴ καὶ αἰὼν συνεχὴς καὶ ἀΐδιος ὑπάρχει τῷ Θεῷ). Ibid, Cap.9:—"The whole life, or entire being," (τὸν ἄπαντα αἰῶνα). De Cœlo, Lib. I., Cap. 10:—"An entire existence" (τὸν ἄπαντα αἰῶνα). Ib., Lib. II., Cap. 1:—"The complete heaven is one and eternal (ἀΐδιος), having no beginning nor end of a whole existence or being," (ἀρχὴν μὲν καὶ τελευτὴν οὐκ ἔχων τοῦ παντὸς αἰῶνος). (See p. 22, "Etymology.") De Part. An. Lib. I., Cap. 5:—"Entire life," (τὸν ἄπαντα αἰῶνα). Rhetor., Lib. I., Cap. 13: —"Life would forsake them numbering, (that is, counting duties of legislators),"—"ὑπολείποι γὰρ δὴ ὁ αἰὼν διαριθμοῦντας." In Phys., Lib. VIII., he quotes from Empedocles whether motion be eternal (ἀΐδιος) and declares that of certain things, life (*aiōn*) is not permanent.

. . . ᾗ μὲν ἓν ἐκ πλεόνων μεμάθηκε φύεσθαι·
ἩΙ δὲ πάλιν διαφύντος ἑνός, πλέον' ἐκτελέθουσι,
Τῇ μὲν γίγνονταί τε, καὶ οὐ σφίσιν ἔμπεδος αἰών

Aristotle (384 B. C.) used the word several times. He

---

28 Cousin quotes the whole of the Commentary by Olympiodorus in his translation of Plato's Gorgias, Vol. III.

speaks of the existence or duration (*aiōn*) of the earth;[29] of an unlimited *aiōnos*;[30] and of "an eternal (*aïdion*) *aiōn*" (or being) "pertaining to God." The fact that Aristotle found it necessary to add *aïdios* to *aiōn* to ascribe eternity to God demonstrates that he found no sense of eternity in the word *aiōn*, and utterly discards the idea that he held the word to mean endless duration, even admitting that he derived it, or supposed the ancients did, from *aei ōn*,—according to the opinion of some lexicographers. A similar use of the word appears in De Cælo.[31] "The entire heaven is one and eternal (*aïdios*) having neither beginning nor end of an entire *aiōn*." In the same work [32] occurs the famous passage where Aristotle has been said to describe the derivation of the word, which we have quoted on page 22:—*Aiōn estin, apo tou aei einai.*

Mr. Goodwin well observes that the word had existed a thousand years before Aristotle's day, and that he had no knowledge of its origin, and poorer facilities for tracing it than many a scholar of the present possesses. "While, therefore, we would regard an opinion of Aristotle on the derivation of an ancient word, with the respect due to extensive learning and venerable age, still we must bear in mind that his opinion is not indisputable authority." Mr. Goodwin proceeds to affirm that Aristotle does not apply *aei ōn* to duration but to God, and that (as we have shown)[33] a human existence is an *aiōn*. Completeness, whether brief or protracted, is his idea. As Aristotle employed it "*aiōn* did not contain the meaning of eternity."[34]

In De Mundo,[35] Aristotle says:—"The stars, sun, and also the moon moving in most perfect measures from one *aiōn* to another *aiōn*." Now, even if Aristotle had said that the word was at first derived from two words that signify always being, his own use of it demonstrates that it had not that meaning then (B. C. 350). Again,[36] he says of the earth, "All these

---

[29] De Mundo, Cap. 5.
[31] Lib. II., Cap. 1.
[33] Etymology.
[35] De Mundo, Cap. 5.
[30] Metaph., Lib. XIV.
[32] Ib., Lib. I., Cap. 9. See also Cap. 10.
[34] Chris. Exam.
[36] Ibid.

things seem to be done for her good, in order to maintain safety during her *aiōnos*," duration, or life. And still more to the purpose is his language concerning God's existence,[37] "Life and *an aiōn* continuous and eternal." Here the word *aïdios*, (eternal) is employed to qualify *aiōn* and impart to it what it had not of itself, the sense of eternal. Aristotle could be guilty of no such language as "an eternal eternity." Had the word *aiōn* contained the idea of eternity in his time, or in his mind, he would not have added *aïdios*. "For the limit enclosing the time of the life of every man, . . . is called his continuous existence, *aiōn*. On the same principle, the limit of the whole heaven, and the limit inclosing the univer-sal system, is the divine, an immortal, ever-existing *aiōn*, de-riving the name *aiōn* from ever-existing, (*aei on*)."[38] In eleven out of twelve instances in the works of Aristotle, *aiōn* is used either doubtfully, or in a manner similar to the instance above cited, (from one *aiōn* to another, that is, from one age to another), but in this last instance it is perfectly clear that an *aiōn* is only without end when it is described by an adjec-tive like *aïdios*, whose meaning is endless. It is a matter of indifference how the word originated, after hearing from Aris-totle himself that created objects exist from one *aiōn* to an-other, and that the existence of the eternal God cannot be described by a word so feeble, but must have the addition of another that expresses endless duration. *Aiōn* only obtains the force of eternal duration by being reënforced by words meaning immortal.[39]

In most cases the word is enlarged by descriptive adjec-tives. Æschylus calls Jupiter "king of the never-ceasing *aiōn*," and Aristotle expressly states in one case that the *aiōn* of heaven "has neither beginning nor end," and in another instance he calls man's life his *aiōn*, and the *aiōn* of heaven "immortal." If *aiōn* denotes eternity, why add "neither beginning nor end,"

---

[37] Metaph. Lib. XIV.   [38] See Etymology, p. 22.
[39] De Part. Animal., Lib. I; Rhetor., Lib. I.; Phys. VIII. (quoting from Empedocles).

or "immortal," to extend its meaning? These quotations unanswerably show that *aiōn* in the Classics never means eternity unless a qualifying word or subject connected with it add to its intrinsic value.

Says Dr. Beecher:—"In Rome there were certain periodical games known as the *secular* games, from the Latin *seculum*, a period, or age. The historian, Herodian, writing in Greek, calls these *aiōnian* games, that is, periodical, occurring at the end of a seculum. It would be singular, indeed, to call them eternal or everlasting games. Cremer, in his masterly Lexicon of New Testament Greek, states the general meaning of the word to be 'belonging to the *aiōn*.'" Herodotus, Isocrates, Xenophon, Sophocles and Diodorus Siculus use the word in precisely the same way. Diodorus Siculus says *ton apeiron aiōna*, "indefinite time."

It appears, then, that the Classic Greek writers, for more than six centuries before the Septuagint was written, used the noun *aiōn* and its adjective, but never once in the sense of endless duration. When, therefore, the Seventy translated the Hebrew Scriptures into Greek, what meaning must they have intended to give to these words? It is not possible, it is absolutely insupposable, that they used them with any other meaning than that which they had held in the antecedent Greek literature. As the Hebrew word meaning horse was rendered by a Greek word meaning horse, as each Hebrew word was exchanged for a Greek word denoting precisely the same thing, so the terms expressive of duration in Hebrew became Greek terms expressing similar duration. The translators consistently render *olam* by *aiōn*, both denoting indefinite duration.

We have shown (pp. 11-12) that the idea of eternity had not entered the Hebrew mind when the Old Testament was written. How, then, could it employ terms expressive of endless duration? We have now shown that the Greek literature uniformly understands the word in the sense of limited duration. This teaches us exactly how the word was taken at the time the Septuagint was prepared, and shows us how to read the Old Testament understandingly.

When at length the idea of eternity was cognized by the human mind, probably first by the Greeks, what word did they employ to represent the idea? Did they regard *aiōn-aiōnion* as adequate? Not at all, but Plato and Aristotle and others employ *aïdios*, and distinctly use it in contrast with our mooted word. We have instanced Aristotle,[39] "The entire heaven is one and eternal (*aïdios*) having neither beginning nor end of a complete *aiōn*, (life, or duration)." In the same chapter *aïdiotes* is used to mean eternity.

Plato[40] calls the gods *aïdion*, and their essence *aïdion*, in contrast with temporal matters, which are *aiōnios*. *Aïdios*, then, is the favorite word descriptive of endless duration in the Greek writers contemporary with the Septuagint. *Aiōn* is never thus used.

Mr. Goodwin well observes:—"Those lexicographers who assign eternity as one of the meanings of *aiōn* uniformly appeal for proofs to either theological, Hebrew or Rabbinical Greek, or some species of Greek subsequent to the age of the Seventy, if not subsequent to the age of the apostles, so far as I can ascertain. I do not know of an instance in which any lexicographer has produced the usage of *ancient* classical Greek in evidence that *aion* means eternity. Ancient Classical Greek rejects it altogether. . . " By "ancient" he means the Greek literature antecedent to the LXX. He thus concludes his conscientious investigation of the seven oldest Greek Classics that he examined, line by line, "*Aiōn* in these writers never expresses positive eternity." [41]

Thus it appears that when the Seventy began their work of giving the world a Greek version of the Old Testament that should convey the exact sense of the Hebrew Bible, they must have used *aiōn* and its derivatives and reduplications in the

---

[39] De Cælo, Lib. II, Cap. 1.   [40] Quoting from Timæus Locrus.
[41] Chris. Exam.

sense in which they then were used. Endless duration is not the meaning the words had in Greek literature at that time. Therefore they cannot have that meaning in the Old Testament Greek. Nothing can be plainer than that Greek Literature at the time the Hebrew Old Testament was rendered into the Greek Septuagint did not give to *aiōn* the meaning of endless duration, so that we must take up the Old Testament predisposed to give to the word, wherever it occurs, and in all its forms, the sense of limited duration. And as we trace it through the Old Testament we shall see that it is used thus, as in the Classics, and as defined by Lexicographers and Critics.[42]

---

[42] Professor Clarke, after surveying all our citations, admits that in the poets *aiōn* means life, and is nearly equivalent to *bios*, but he thinks that from the time of Plato there was a complete substitution of the metaphysical meaning of eternity. We have never seen any evidence of the extraordinary assumption that the great philosopher accomplished so stupendous a feat as to revolutionize the meaning of a word—one which would seem to every philologist quite impossible. Until demonstrated, students must accredit Plato with employing the word as he found it. Besides, as we now proceed to show, the LXX. disregarded the example attributed to him by Prof. Clarke, and used the word as the other Classics had always done. In assuming that Plato endeavored to foist the sense of eternity into *aiōn*, Professor Clarke makes the strongest kind of argument against his own position, for even so great a literary autocrat as Plato could not make the meaning stick, inasmuch as subsequent writers refused to recognize his authority, but continued to employ the word as their predecessors had done. Had Plato—as he did not—infused eternal duration into *aiōn*, in his own writings, its inherent sense asserted itself the moment Plato's influence was withdrawn! But our quotations show that the great philosopher's custom harmonized with that of preceding writers.

NOTE.—Having submitted the proofs of the chapter relating to the Classics to President White, he kindly furnished this important correction:

On page 52, Prof. Clark seems to be singularly in error. I refer to the quotation from Erinna. I am aware that some writers think that Erinna addressed her ode to *Rhome* (Might). The weight of authority is on the other side. The word *aiōn* is not used even in the sense of age by any Greek writer so early as Erinna (610 B. C.). The poem was probably written to the "Genius of *Rome*" (city) and *not* by the Erinna who was Sappho's pupil (610 B. C.), but by another poetess of the same name who lived about 300

B. C., or at least in the time of Rome's supremacy. Others who take the same or a similar view attribute the poem to *Melinna*, a poetess who lived about the same time. *I* discovered my error in this matter after several months' looking—I could give you quite a history in this connection. I will cite only one authority:—Moebius, in his "Fragments of Anacreon, Sappho and Erinna," inserts this poem, but says it is *not* by the contemporary of Sappho. Moebius' notes are in Latin. I will translate somewhat freely:— "Stobaeus has preserved for us this most elegant ode 'on Rome,' and he calls it the ode of Melinna (or Melinnus) or, rather of Erinna, the Lesbian: *this Erinna* was not the contemporary of Sappho, but she must have lived at a later time, when Rome had arrived at the zenith of her power . . . . . *for*, those are not at all to be believed who think that the *goddess* 'Might,' and not the city, Rome, is celebrated in this Ode." The author (Moebius) refers for *his* authority to Jacob's "Lyrische Blumen," p. 227. Also to F. Th. Welker in Creuzern Meletem, Vol. II., p. 18, etc., etc. Welker is a first-class authority. This is a matter of first importance.

USAGE.—II.—*THE OLD TESTAMENT.*

The Pentateuch was rendered into Greek at about the time of the return from the Babylonish captivity, and the entire Old Testament was combined in one collection about 384-347 B. C.,[1] somewhere near the time of the death of Plato, who may have seen it.

It is difficult to realize how thoroughly Greek in their literature were the Jews at the time of Christ. Says Geikie:[2]—

---

[1] Prideaux, (Connection, Vol. III., Part ii., Book 1.,) says, 300-200 B. C.; but more recent and better authorities say 384-347 B. C., during the reign of Ptolemy Philadelphus. It was immediately introduced into Palestine from Alexandria, and became the common Bible of the Jews, who at that time spoke the Aramaic. It was from this version that Jesus and the Apostles almost uniformly quoted.

[2] The Life and Words of Christ, by Cunningham Geikie, D. D.

"Even in the days of the Syrian kings, Palestine had been encircled by Greek towns and cities, and the immigration of Greek settlers had, in Herod's day, made the towns of the Philistine coast and of the Decapolis much more Greek than Jewish. . . . Greek had become the court dialect of the Empire, as French was that of Europe in the days of Louis XIV.; and hence it was universally favored and spoken by the upper classes in Herod's dominions. It seemed as if the throne of David existed only to spread heathenism!" It was because of this state of things that the Jews in Palestine were as familiar with the Greek version of the Old Testament as with the Hebrew Scriptures, and hence Christ and his apostles almost invariably quoted from the LXX. To say that they gave to Greek words a meaning different from that which those words carried in the Classic Greek, spoken and read all about them, is to contradict the self-evident facts of the case. Of course the Seventy gave to all Greek words the same meaning they had in the Classic Greek. To ascertain just what the Greek Old Testament means by *aiōn*, or any other word, we need only learn its meaning in contemporaneous Greek. The Seventy would as soon have rendered the Hebrew word for horse by a Greek word meaning fly, as they would have used *aiōn* for endless duration, if, as we have shown, and shall show is the fact, antecedent and contemporaneous Greek literature used it to denote limited duration.

It cannot, then, be denied or doubted that the word under discussion has the same meaning in the Greek version of the Old Testament, that it bore in preceding and contemporaneous Greek literature.[3] And in giving the world a Greek version of the Old Testament that should convey the exact sense of the Hebrew Bible, the Seventy must have used *aiōn* in the sense in which *olam* was used, inasmuch as it is its invariable equivalent; and as endless duration is not the meaning the word had in Greek literature—as we have shown—therefore the

---

[3] The Greek Old Testament is the best of all lexicons of the Greek equivalents of Hebrew words.

word cannot have that meaning in the Old Testament Greek.
Nothing can be plainer than that Greek literature, at the time
the Hebrew Old Testament was rendered into the Greek Septuagint did not give to *aiōn* the meaning of endless duration,
and it is therefore self-evident that the Old Testament must
employ the word in the sense of indefinite duration; otherwise
the Old Testament would mislead its readers.

Rev. E. S. Goodwin, speaking of the Septuagint, observes :[4]
—"These translators were Greek scholars. Jews or Gentiles,
they must have been acquainted with Greek literature, or they
could not have been competent to the work of translation. , In
translating, they made use of Greek words in a classical sense
wherever they could. In selecting a Greek word to represent
a Hebrew word, they selected one which sustained, in true
Greek, a general meaning, as near as might be, to the sense
which they believed to exist in the Hebrew word. In translating a Hebrew word sustaining several meanings, they selected
for the purpose, as nearly as possible, a Greek term
sustaining the same different senses. Their Greek words
ought to be understood in their classical sense, unless it should
be in evidence that they employed them, in the instances in
question, in some peculiar Hebrew-Greek sense; due allowance
being made for the different idioms of the two languages, and
for those shades of difference which exist in words most
nearly correspondent to each other in different languages. The
Seventy uniformly employ αἰὼν or αἰώνιος to represent what
they understood עוֹלָם to signify in Hebrew; so uniformly, that
to all purposes of the present investigation it may be said
they always do so. There are terms in the Greek language
which express eternity and eternal, besides αἰὼν and αἰώνιος,
whether these latter express these ideas or not. But those
other terms are never employed in translating עוֹלָם. The
Seventy met with the word עוֹלָם in the Hebrew Scriptures;
they selected αἰὼν and αἰώνιος, as the proper terms by which

---

4 Chris. Exam., March, 1831.

to translate it; they adhered to these words for this purpose with a scrupulous pertinacity. The inference is direct, that they believed this Hebrew term to bear an import as nearly equal to that of these Greek words in classical Greek, as the idioms of the two languages would admit. Whatever, then, was the import of αἰὼν or αἰὼνιος in true Greek in their age, we must believe that such was the meaning of עוֹלָם in their minds, and (considering their favorable circumstances) that such was its true meaning, with proper allowances as above stated."

Before proceeding to exhibit the usage of the word in the Old Testament, let us pause a moment on the brink of our investigation to speak of the utter absurdity of the idea that God has suspended the immortal welfare of millions of souls on the meaning of a single equivocal word. Had he intended to teach endless punishment by any word, that word would have been so explicit and uniform and frequent that no mortal could mistake its meaning. It would have been guarded from first to last with strictest care, and would have stood unique and peculiar among words. It would no more be found conveying a limited meaning in any instance than is the sacred name of Jehovah applied to any finite being. Instead of denoting every degree of duration, as it does, it never would have meant less than eternity. The thought that God has suspended the question of man's final destiny on such a word would seem too preposterous to be entertained by any reflecting mind, did we not know that such an idea is held by Christians. And yet, endless duration is never expressed or implied in the Old Testament by *aiōn* or any of its derivatives except in instances where it acquires that meaning from the subject with which it is connected, as the word great signifies infinite when it describes Deity. Out of five hundred and four [5] occurrences of the disputed word in the Old Testament, about four hundred denote limited duration, so that the great

---

[5] The noun 394 times, and the adjective 110 times; and all but four are translations of *olam*.

preponderance of Old Testament usage fully agrees with that of
the Greek Classics. The remaining instances follow the rule
given · by the best lexicographers,—that it only means endless
when it derives its meaning of endlessness from the nature of
the subject with which it is connected.[6]

Dr. Beecher[7] remarks that the sense of endless given to
the aionian phraseology "fills the Old Testament with contra-
dictions, for it would make it declare the absolute eternity of
systems which it often and emphatically declares to be temporary. Nor can it be said that *aiŏnios* denotes lasting as long
as the nature of things permits. The Mosaic ordinances
might have lasted at least to the end of the world, but did
not. Moreover, on this principle the exceptions to the true
sense of the word exceed its proper use; for in the majority
of cases in the Old Testament, *aiŏnios* is applied to that
which is limited and temporary."

Let us first consider the noun as it is used in the Old
Testament. Waiving the passages where it is applied to
God, and where by accommodation it may be allowed to
imply endlessness, just as great applied to God means infinity,
let us consult the general usage.[8] Eccl. i: 10, "Is there anything whereof it may be said, See, this is new! it hath been
already of *old time*, which was before us." Ps. xxv: 6,
"Remember, O Lord, thy tender mercies and thy loving kindness; for they have been *ever of old*." Ps. cxix: 52, "I remembered thy judgments *of old*, O Lord; and have comforted
myself." Isa. xlvi: 9, "Remember the former things *of old*."
Isa. lxiv: 4, "Since the *beginning of the world*." Jer.
xxviii: 8, "The prophets that have been before me and before
thee *of old* prophesied both against many countries, and
against great kingdoms, of war, and of evil, and of pestilence."
Jer. ii: 20, "For *of old time* I have broken thy yoke, and
burst thy bands." Prov. viii: 23, "I (wisdom) was set up from

---

[6] See pp. 9-10.   [7] Hist. Fut. Ret.
[8] The English words representing *aiŏn* are printed in italics.

everlasting, from the beginning, or ever the earth was."
Here everlasting and "before the world was," are in apposition.
Ps. lxxiii: 12, "Behold, these are the ungodly, who prosper
in the *world*." Deut. xxxii: 7, "Remember the days *of old*."
Ezek. xxvi: 20, "The people of *old time*." Ps. cxliii: 3,
"Those who have been *long* dead." Same in Lam. iii: 6.
Amos. ix. 11, "Days *of old*." Isa. li: 9, "Generations *of old*." -
Micah. vii: 14, "Days *of old*." Same in Malachi iii: 4.
Ps. xlviii :14, "For this God is our God *for ever and ever*: he will
be our guide even unto death." This plural form denotes no
longer than "even unto death." Christ's kingdom is prophesied as
destined to endure *"forever," "without end,"* etc. (Dan. ii: 44;
Isa. lix: 21; Ps. cx: 4; Isa. ix: 7; Ps. lxxxix: 29.) Now if anything is taught in the Bible, it is that Christ's kingdom shall
end. In I. Cor. xv it is expressly and explicitly declared
that Jesus shall surrender the kingdom to God the Father,
that his reign shall entirely cease. Hence, when we read in
such passages as Dan. ii: 44, that Christ's kingdom shall
stand *forever*, we must understand that the forever denotes
the reign of Messias bounded by "the end" when God shall
be "all in all."

Servants were declared to be bound *forever*, when all servants were emancipated every fifty years. Thus, in Deut. xv:
16-17, we read, "And it shall be, if he say unto thee, I will not
go away from thee; because he loveth thee and thine house,
because he is well with thee, then thou shalt take an awl, and
thrust it through his ear unto the door, and he shall be thy servant *forever*." And yet we are told (Lev. xxv: 10, 39-41), "And ye
shall hallow the fiftieth year, and proclaim liberty throughout
all the land unto all the inhabitants thereof—it shall be a jubilee unto you; and ye shall return every man unto his posses-
sions, and ye shall return every man unto his family. And if
thy brother that dwelleth with thee be waxen poor, and be
sold unto thee; thou shalt not compel him to serve as a bond
servant, but as a hired servant, and as a sojourner, he shall be
with thee, and shall serve unto the year of jubilee; and then
shall he depart from thee, both he and his children with him, and

shall return unto his own family and unto the possession of his father shall he return." This forever, at the utmost, could only be forty-nine years and three hundred and sixty-four days and some odd hours.

And certainly no one will ascribe endless duration to *aiōn* in the following passages:—II. Sam. vii : 16, "And thine house and thy kingdom shall be established *for ever* before thee—thy throne shall be established *for ever*." II. Sam. vii : 29, "There- fore now let it please thee to bless the house of thy servant, that it may continue *forever* before thee—for thou, O Lord God, hast spoken it; and with thy blessing let the house of thy servant be blessed *for ever*. This is the house and kingdom and throne of David." I. K. ii : 45, "And king Solomon shall be blessed, and the throne of David shall be established before the Lord *forever*." I K. ix : 5, "Then I will establish the throne of thy kingdom upon Israel *for ever*, as I promised to David thy father, saying, There shall not fail thee a man upon the throne of Israel." I. Chron. xvii : 27, Now, therefore, let it please thee to bless the house of thy servant, that it may be before thee *for ever*; for thou blessest, O Lord, and it shall be blessed *for ever*." I. Chron. xxviii : 4, "Howbeit, the Lord God of Israel chose me before all the house of my father to be king over Israel *for ever*; for he hath chosen Judah to be the ruler; and of the house of Judah, the house of my father; and among the sons of my father he liked me to make me king over all Israel." II. Chron. xiii : 5, "Ought ye not to know that the Lord God of Israel gave the kingdom over Israel to David *for ever*, even to him and his sons by a covenant of salt?" Ps. lxxxix : 3-4, "I have made a covenant with my chosen, I have sworn unto David my servant. Thy seed will I establish *for ever*, and build up thy throne to all generations. Selah." Ps. lxxxix : 36, "His seed shall endure *for ever*, and his throne as the sun before me." Ps. lxxxix : 37, "It shall be established *for ever* as the moon, and as a faithful witness in heaven. Selah." Ezek. xxxvii : 25, "And they shall dwell in the land that I have given unto Jacob my servant, where- in your fathers have dwelt; and they shall dwell therein, even they and their children, and their children's children *for ever*; and my servant David shall be their prince *for ever*." I. Sam. xiii : 13, "And Samuel said to Saul, Thou hast done foolishly; thou hast not kept the commandment of the Lord thy God, which he commanded thee; for now would the Lord have established thy kingdom upon Israel *for ever*." Jer. xxxi : 40, "And the whole valley of the dead bodies, and of the ashes, and all the fields unto the brook of Kidron, unto the corner of the horse gate toward the east, shall be holy unto the Lord; it shall not be plucked up, nor thrown down any more *for ever*."

See also II. Sam. vii : 13, 16, 25, 26, xxii : 51; I. K. ii : 33; I. Chron. xvii : 12,14, 14, 23, xxii : 10, xxviii :7; Ps. xviii :50, lxxxix : 4, and cxxxii :12; Ex. xxxii :13; Josh. xiv :9; I. Chr. xxviii : 7; Jud. ii : 1; II. Chron. vii :3; Ps. cv : 8; Gen. xiii : 15; I. Chron. xxviii : 4, 7, 8; Ezek. xxxvii : 25; Jer. vii : 7,7; II. Sam. vii : 24; I. Chron. xvii : 22; Joel iii : 20; II. K. xxi : 7; II. Chron. xxxiii : 4; Ps. xlviii : 8; Jer. xvii : 25; I. Chron. xxiii : 25; Isa. xxiii :7; I. K. ix : 3; II. Chron. xxx : 8; Ezek. xxxvii : 26, 28; II. Chron. vii : 16; Ex. xix :9, and xl :15; I. Chron. xxiii : 13,25; I. Chron. xv : 2; Lev. iii : 17; II. Chron. ii : 4; Ex. xii : 24; Josh. iv : 7; Am. i : 11; Isa. xiii : 20; Isa. xxxiii : 20; xxxiv : 10; I. K. x : 9; II. Chron. ix : 8; Ps. cii : 28; Ezek. xliii : 7. Certainly in all these texts a limited duration is the utmost that the language will bear. And these are specimen passages of the prevailing sense of the term throughout the Old Testament, as the reader may easily ascertain.

The adjective is used in the same sense as the noun in these and other passages:—Gen. ix : 12, 16, xvii : 8, 13, 19; Numb. xxv : 13; Ex. xii : 14, 17, xxvii : 21, xxviii : 43, xxix : 28, xxx : 21, xxxi : 16, 17; Lev. vi : 18, 22, vii : 34, 36, x : 15, xvi : 29, 31, 34, xvii : 7, xxiii : 14, 31, 41, xxiv : 3, 8, 9; Numb. x : 8, xv : 15, xviii : 8, 11, 19, 23, xix : 10, 21; II. Sam. xxiii : 5; I. Chron. xvi : 17; Isa. xxiv : 5; Ezek. xvi : 60; Ps. lxxvii : 5; Isa. lxiii : 11; Jer. vi : 16, xviii : 15, xxii : 15; Isa. lviii : 12, lxi : 4; Ezek. xxvi : 20; Prov. xxii : 28, xxiii : 10;

Ezek. xxxvi: 2, xxxv: 5; Isa. liv: 8; Jer. v: 22, xviii: 16, xxv: 9, 12; Ezek. xxxv: 9; Jer. xx: 11, xxiii: 40, li: 39; Micah ii: 9.

We will quote some of the foregoing texts :—"And ye shall observe the feast of unleavened bread; for in this self-same day have I brought your armies out of the land of Egypt— therefore shall ye observe this day in your generations by an ordinance *for ever*." "And thou shalt command the children of Israel, that they bring thee pure oil-olive beaten for the light, to cause the lamp to burn *always*." "In the tabernacle of the congregation without the vail, which is before the tes- timony, Aaron and his sons shall order it from evening to morning before the Lord—it shall be a statute *for ever* unto their generations on behalf of the children of Israel." "And they shall be upon Aaron and upon his sons, when they come in unto the tabernacle of the congregation, or when they come near unto the altar to minister in the holy place; that they bear not iniquity and die—it shall be a statute *for ever* unto him and his seed after him." "Hast thou not marked the *old* way which wicked men have trodden?" "Fear ye not me— saith the Lord—will ye not tremble at my presence, which have placed the sand for the bound of the sea by a *perpetual* decree, that it cannot pass it; and though the waves thereof toss themselves, yet can they not prevail: though they roar, yet can they not pass over it." All of the above references are similarly used. To render the word eternal will show how absurd such a definition would be in the following passages :[9]—"I will give unto thee, and thy seed after thee, the land wherein thou art a stranger, all the land of Canaan, for an *eternal* possession." "And thou shalt anoint them as thou didst their father, that they may minister unto me in the priest's office; for their anointing shall surely be a priesthood through the *eternity*." "Then his master shall bring him to the door, or unto the door-posts, and his master shall bore his ear through with an awl, and he shall serve him through the *eternity*."

---

[9] Gen. xvii: 8; Ex. xl: 15; xxi: 6; Jonah ii: 5-6. The Greek gives the adjective in Jonah ii, but the accurate rendering of the Hebrew is forever.

" The waters compassed me about—even to the soul;
The weeds were wrapped about my head,
I went down to the bottoms of the mountains;
The earth with her *eternal* bars was about me."

Still further do the subjoined texts demonstrate the impropriety of the popular rendering, which would compel us to read [10]—"The Lord shall reign *to* the *eternity*, and *during* the *eternity*, and *longer*." "And they that be wise shall shine as the brightness of the firmament; and they that turn many to righteousness as the stars through the *eternities* and *longer*." "And we will walk in the name of Jehovah our God through the eternity and *longer*." But substitute ages and the sense is perfect. Ex. xv: 18, "The Lord shall reign from *age to age*, and beyond all the *ages*"; Dan. xii: 3, "Through the *ages* and beyond them all"; Micah iv: 5, "Through the *ages* and beyond."

No one can read the Old Testament unbiased, and fail to see that the word has a great range of meaning, bearing some such relation to duration as the word great does to size. We say God is infinite when we call him the great God, not because great means infinite, but because God is infinite. The *aiōnion* God is of eternal duration, but the *aiōnion* smoke of Idumea has expired, and the *aiōnion* hills will one day crumble, and all merely aionian things will cease to be. Prof. David Swing says:—"There are many 'forevers' in public thought:—(1) The complimentary forever, as O King, live for ever! but the King will not do it. (2) The forever of friendship, as I shall love you forever. (3) The forever of rhetoric, as the smoke of her torment ascends forever. (4) The forever of comparison, as one generation passeth away, another generation cometh, but the earth abideth forever. It will do so in comparison with the brief life of the generation, but the earth has no essential eternity given it, for the moment it is compared with the life of God, it becomes the temporary thing, and God the everlasting:

[10] Ex xv: 18; Dan. xii: 3; Micah. iv: 5.

> The sun, himself, shall fade,
> The starry worlds shall fall
> And through a vast eternity,
> Shall God be all in all."

While it is a rule of language that adjectives qualify and describe nouns, it is no less true that nouns sometimes modify adjectives. A tall plant, a tall dog, a tall man, and a tall tree are of different degrees of length, though the different nouns are described by the same adjective. The adjective is in each instance modified by its noun, just as the æonian bars that held Jonah three days, and the æonian priesthood of Aaron already ended, and the æonian hills yet to be destroyed, and æonian punishment, always proportioned to human guilt, are of different degrees of length. The adjective is modified and its length is determined by the noun with which it is connected. Thus, in Gen. xxi: 33, God is æonian; Gen. xvii: 8, Canaan is an æonian possession; Numb. xxv: 13, the Aaronic priesthood is æonian; in Jonah ii: 6, three days are æonian; Proverbs xxii: 28 calls the old boundaries of land æonian; in Hab. iii: 6, the hills are æonian, so that the word possesses all degrees of meaning, from three days to strict eternity, according to the noun that accompanies it. How absurd, then, to assume that it must mean endless when applied to punishment.

Prof. Tayler Lewis says,[11] " 'One generation passeth away, and another generation cometh; but the earth abideth forever.' This certainly indicates not an endless eternity in the strictest sense of the word, but only a future of unlimited length. Ex. xxxi: 16, 'Wherefore the children of Israel shall keep the Sabbath, to observe the Sabbath throughout their generations, for a perpetual covenant.' *Aiōn* here would seem to be taken as a hyperbolical term for indefinite or unmeasured duration." Where the context demands it, as "I live forever," spoken of God, he says it means endless duration, for "it is the subject to which it is applied that forces to this, and not any etymological necessity in the word itself." He adds that *olam* and

---

[11] Note on Eccl. i: 4; Lange's Com. pp. 45-50.

aiōn in the plural, ages and ages of ages, demonstrate that neither of the words, of itself, denotes eternity. He admits that they are used to give an idea of eternity, but that applied to God and his kingdom, the ages are finite. Prof. L. was eminently learned and as eminently orthodox.

Canaan was given to the Jews for an everlasting possession, Gen. xvii: 8, xlviii: 4; the hills are everlasting, Gen. xlix: 26; the priesthood of Aaron is everlasting, Numb. xxv: 13; the Jewish law was to be everlasting, Lev. xvi: 34; the mountains, though everlasting, were scattered, Hab. iii: 6; Gehazi was to be a leper forever, II. Kings v: 27; and certain bondmen were to be servants forever, Deut. xv: 17, Lev. xxv: 46; the land was given to Abram forever, Gen. xiii: 15; Jerusalem was to remain forever, Jer. xvii: 25, xxxi: 40, Ps. xlviii: 8; Jonah was in the fish three days, and after he came out he declared "Earth with her bars was about me forever," Jonah ii: 6; none was to pass through the land of Idumea forever and ever, Isa. xxxiv: 10; and the Jews were to dwell in their land forever and ever, Jer. vii: 7. And yet the Jews have lost their eternal excellency; Aaron and his sons have ceased from their priest- hood; the Mosaic system is superseded by Christianity; the Jews no longer possess Canaan; David and his house have lost the throne of Israel; the Jewish temple is destroyed, and Jeru- salem is no longer the holy city; the servants who were to be bondmen forever are all free from their masters; Gehazi is cured of his leprosy; the stones are removed from Jordan, and the smoke of Idumea no longer rises; the righteous do not possess the land promised them forever; some of the hills and mountains have fallen, and the tooth of time will one day gnaw the last of them into dust; the fire has expired from the Jewish altar; Jonah has escaped from his imprisonment; all these and numerous other eternal, everlasting things—things that were to last forever, and to which the various æonian words were applied—have now ended, and if these hundreds of instances must denote limited duration why should the few times in which the same word is connected with punishment have any other meaning? Even if endless duration were the intrinsic meaning of the word, all intelligent readers of the Bible would perceive that the word must be employed to denote limited duration in the passages above cited. And surely in the very few times in which it is connected with punishment it must have a similar meaning. For who administers this punishment? Not a monster, not an infinite devil, but a God of love and mercy; and the same common sense that would forbid us to give the word the meaning of endless duration, were that its literal meaning, when we see it applied to what we know has ended, would forbid us to give it that meaning when applied to the dealings of an infinite Father with an erring and beloved child. But when we interpret it in the light of its general usage out of the Old Testament, and perceive that it only has the sense of endless when the subject compels it, as when referring to God, we cannot allow that it denotes endless duration when describing God's punishments.

Let the reader consider further illustrations of the Bible usage of the word. Gen. vi: 4, "There were giants in the earth in those days; and also after that, when the sons of God came in unto the daughters of men, and they bare children to them, the same became mighty men which were *of old*, men of renown." Gen. ix: 12, God's covenant with Noah was "for *perpetual* generations." Gen. ix: 16, the rainbow is the token of "the *everlasting* covenant" between God and "all flesh that is upon the earth." Gen. xiii: 15, God gave the land to Abraham and his seed "*forever.*" Dr. T. Clowes says of this passage that it signifies the duration of human life, and he adds, "Let no one be surprised that we use the word olam (*aiōn*) in *this limited sense. This is one of the most usual significations of the Hebrew olam and the Greek aiōn.*" In Isa. lviii: 12 it is rendered "*old*" and "*foundations*": "And they that shall be of thee shall build the *old* waste places; thou shalt raise up the *foundations* of many generations; and thou shalt be called the repairer of the breach." In Jer. xviii: 15, 16, *ancient* and *perpetual:* "Because my people hath forgotten me, they have burned incense to vanity, and they have caused them to stumble in their ways from the *ancient* paths, to walk in paths, in a way not cast up; to make their land desolate, and a *perpetual* hissing; every one that passeth thereby shall be astonished, and wag his head." Such instances may be cited to an indefinite extent. Ex. xv: 18, "Forever and ever and further."[12] Ex. xii: 17, " And ye shall observe the feast of unleavened bread; for this self-same day have I brought your armies out of the land of Egypt, therefore shall ye observe this day in your generations by an ordinance *forever*." Numb. x: 8, "And the sons of Aaron, the priests, shall blow with the trumpets; and they shall be to you for an ordinance *forever* throughout your gene-rations." "Your generations," here idiomatically stands as the precise equivalent of "forever." Canaan was given as an " *everlasting* possession," (Gen. xvii: 8, xlviii: 4); the hills are *everlasting* (Hab. iii : 6); the priesthood of Aaron (Lev. xxiv : 8, 9; Ex. xl: 15; Numb. xxv: 13; Lev. xvi: 34) was to exist *forever*, and continue through *everlasting* duration; Solo-mon's temple was to last *forever* (I. Chron. xvii: 12), though it has long since ceased to be; slaves were to remain in bond-age *forever* (Lev. xxv: 46), though every fiftieth year all Hebrew servants were to be set at liberty, (Lev. xxv: 10); Jonah suffered an imprisonment behind the *everlasting* bars of earth, (Jon. ii: 6); the smoke of Idumea was to ascend *forever*, (Isa. xxxiv: 10) though it no longer rises; to the Jews God says (Jer. xxxii: 40), "And I will bring an *everlasting* reproach upon you, and a *perpetual* shame, which shall not be forgot-ten," and yet, after the fullness of the Gentiles shall come in, Israel will be restored, (Rom. xi: 25-6.)

Not only in all these and multitudes of other cases does the word mean limited duration, but it is also used in the plural, thus debarring it from the sense of endless, as there can be but one eternity. In Dan. xii: 3 the literal reading, if we allow the word to mean eternity, is, " to *eternities and*

---

[12] τὸν αἰῶνα, καὶ ἐπ᾽ αἰῶνα, καὶ ἔτι.

farther."[13] Micah. iv: 5, "We will walk in the name of the Lord our God to eternity and beyond"; Ex. xv: 18, "From eternity to eternity and further"; Ps. cxix: 43–44, "And take not the word of truth utterly out of my mouth; for I have hoped in thy judgments. So shall I keep thy law continually *forever and ever.*" This is the strongest combination of the æonian phraseology,[14] and yet it is David's promise of fidelity so long as he lives among them that "reproach" him, in "the house of his pilgrimage." Ps. cxlviii: 4–6, "Praise him, ye heaven of heavens, and ye waters that be above the heavens. Let them praise the name of the LORD: for he commanded and they were created. He hath also established them for *ever and ever*: he hath made a decree which shall not pass. The sun and moon, the stars of light, and even the waters above the heavens are established *forever*,"[15] and yet the firmament is one day to become as a folded garment, and the orbs of heaven are to be no more. Endless duration is out of the question in these and many similar instances.

In Lam. v: 19, "forever and ever" is used as the equivalent of "from generation to generation." Joel ii: 26–27, "And ye shall eat in plenty, and be satisfied, and praise the name of the LORD your God, that hath dealt wondrously with you: and my people shall *never* be ashamed. And ye shall know that I am in the midst of Israel, and that I am the Lord your God and none else: and my people shall *never* be ashamed." This is spoken of the Jewish nation. Isa. lx: 15, "Whereas, thou hast been forsaken and hated, so that no man went through thee, I will make thee an *eternal* excellency, a joy of many generations." Here many generations, and eternal, are exact equivalents. I. Sam. i: 22, "But Hannah went not up: for she said unto her husband, I will not go up until the child be weaned, and then I will bring him, that he may appear before the LORD, and there abide *forever*." The remaining of Sam-

---

[13] εἰς τοὺς αἰῶνας, καὶ ἔτι.

[14] εἰς τὸν αἰῶνα καὶ εἰς τὸν αἰῶνα τοῦ αἰῶνος.

[15] εἰς τὸν αἰῶνα καὶ εἰς τὸν αἰῶνα τοῦ αἰῶνος.

uel in the temple was to be *"forever."* II. Kings v: 27, "The leprosy, therefore, of Naaman shall cleave unto thee, and unto thy seed *forever."* Whether the seed of Gehazi is still on earth, the leprosy has departed. Daniel ii: 4, " Then spake the Chaldeans to the king in Syriac, O king, live *forever."* The Chaldean's "Live forever" meant precisely what the French *"Vive,"* and the English "Long live the king" mean. Eternal duration never entered the thought. Jer. xvii: 25, "Then shall there enter into the gates of this city kings and princes sitting upon the throne of David, riding in chariots and on horses; they, and their princes, the men of Judah, and the inhabitants of Jerusalem and this city shall remain *forever."* Eternity was not promised here,—long duration is the extent of the meaning. Josh. iv: 7, "Then ye shall answer them, that the waters of Jordan were cut off before the ark of the covenant of the Lord: when it passed over Jordan, the waters of Jordan were cut off; and these stones shall be for a memorial unto the children of Israel *forever."* These stones are no longer a memorial,—*this* forever has ended.

Forever and ever is applied to the hosts of heaven, or the sun, moon, and stars; to a writing contained in a book; to the smoke that went up from the burning land of Idumea; and to the time the Jews were to dwell in Judea.[16]

Never is applied to the time the sword was to remain in the house of David, and to the time the Jews should experience shame.[17]

Everlasting [18] is applied to God's covenant with the Jews; to the priesthood of Aaron; to the statutes of Moses; to the time the Jews were to possess the land of Canaan; to the mountains and hills; and to the doors of the Jewish temple.[19]

Forever is applied to the duration of man's earthly exis-

[16] Ps. cxlviii: 5-6; Isa. xxx: 8; xxxiv: 10; Jer. vii: 7; xxv: 5.
[17] II. Sam. xii: 10; Joel ii: 26-27.
[18] Univ. Book of Reference, pp. 106-7.
[19] Gen. xvii: 7, 8, 13; xlviii: 4; xlix: 26; Ex. xl: 15; Lev. xvi: 34; Num. xxv: 13; Ps. xxiv: 7; Hab. iii: 6.

tence; to the time a child was to abide in the temple; to the continuance of Gehazi's leprosy; to the duration of the life of David;
to the duration of a king's life; to the duration of the earth;
to the time the Jews were to possess the land of Canaan;
to the time they were to dwell in Jerusalem; to the time a servant was to abide with his master; to the time Jerusalem was
to remain a city; to the duration of the Jewish temple; to
the laws and ordinances of Moses; to the time David was to
be king over Israel; to the throne of Solomon; to the stones
that were set up at Jordan; to the time the righteous were to
inhabit the earth; and to the time Jonah was in the fish's belly.[20]

And yet, the land of Canaan, the Jews' "everlasting possession," has passed from their hands; the covenant of circumcision, an "everlasting covenant," was abolished almost two
thousand years ago; the Jewish atonement (Lev. xvi), an everlasting statute, is abrogated by the atonement of Christ; David
was never to want a man to sit on Israel's throne, but this
æonian line of succession was long ago broken.

Many passages allude to the earth as enduring forever;
to the grave, as man's "long home"; to God's existence, as
"forever," etc. Often the language is equivalent to "to the
ages," or "from age to age," and sometimes eternal duration is
intended, not because the word compels it, but because the
theme treated requires it. It is true that the adjective is applied
to God, Zion, and things intrinsically endless, and thus acquires
from the connected subjects a meaning not inherent in the
word, as in the following passages:—Gen. xxi: 33; Ex. iii: 15;
Job xii: 12; Isa. xl: 28, li: 11, liv: 8, lv: 3, 13, lvi: 5, lx: 15,
19, lxi: 7, 8, lxiii: 12; Ezek. xxxvii: 26; Dan. vii: 27, ix: 24,
xii: 2; Hab. iii: 6; Ps. cxii: 6, cxxxvi: 8. Thus, "And Abraham
planted a grove in Beersheba, and called there on the name of

---

[20] Deut. xv : 17 ; I. Sam. i : 22 ; xxvii : 12; Lev. xxv : 46 ; II. Kings v : 27 ; Job
xl : 4 ; I. Kings i : 31 ; Neh. ii : 3 ; Dan. ii : 4 ; Exod. xiv : 13 ; Ecc. i : 4 ; Ps. civ :
5 ; lxxviii : 69 ; Ezek. xxxvii : 25 ; Gen. xiii : 15 ; Exod. xxxii : 13 ; Josh. xiv : 9 ;
I. Chron. xxiii : 25 ; Jer. xvii : 25 ; Ps. xlviii : 8 ; Jer. xxxi : 40 ; I. Kings viii :
13 ; Num. x : 8 ; xviii : 23 ; I. Chron. xxviii : 4 ; I. Kings ix : 5 ; Josh. iv : 7 ;
Jonah ii : 6 ; Ps. xxxvii : 29.

the Lord, the *everlasting* God." The adjective *aiōnion* is here applied to God, in the sense of eternal, because the nature of God requires it, though, as Knapp and LeClerc say, the author of the language had no definite idea of endless duration when he employed the term. The word is used in the same way here:—"The Lord God of your fathers, the God of Abraham, the God of Isaac, and the God of Jacob, hath sent me unto you: this is my name *forever*, and this is my memorial unto all generations." "All generations" is put as the equivalent of forever, here, showing that the word is employed rhetorically rather than accurately. The word acquires an added force, from its connections, to its original strength in the foregoing passages, and in others that it is unnecessary to cite. The reader can consult them from the above references.

The usage of the term as a plural, as having a beginning and an ending, and its application to so many subjects that have ended or must end, compels us to believe that its intrinsic meaning is a duration determined by its surroundings, as Alex. Campbell, Scarlett, Stuart, Dr. Taylor, Schleusner, and others declare, [21] "to be determined by the persons or things spoken of, and the scope of the subjects." And if the word derives its meaning from the subject with which it is connected, surely it must denote limited duration when related to the punishments administered by a merciful Father to his weak and erring children, especially, when, as we shall see in the New Testament use of the word, that punishment is described by a term that signifies to "chasten, correct, prune."

If Jonah could say, "Out of the belly of hell cried I, earth with her bars was about me *forever*,"—if he was, as he says he was, in "hell forever," when only three days in the fish, is it not evident that the word does not of itself signify an unlimited duration, and is it not further evident that when we see it applied to the consequences of sin we must give it a meaning that shall harmonize with the Divine character, and the nature of just punishment? Defining it thus, who can give one reason

---

[21] See Lexicography in this volume.

for understanding it as meaning endless? Considering who
inflicts punishment, it is morally more absurd to give to everlasting the meaning of endless when applied to it, than it is
mathematically absurd to say that Jonah's forever—seventy-
two hours,—was literally endless. If Canaan was to pass from
the possession of the Jews; if the hills were to be melted, and
the priesthood of Aaron to end; the Jewish law to cease;
the mountains to be destroyed; Gehazi's leprosy no longer to
last; the bondmen's chains to be melted; Abraham to lose possession of his land; Jerusalem to be destroyed, and Jonah to
remain in the fish only three days when all were to be everlasting,
eternal, forever,—what conceivable reason is there for supposing
that punishment shall last forever, when only the same qualifying words are applied to it?

Canon Farrar observes: [22]—"Thus in the Old Testament
aiōn, aiōnios and many such varieties of expression (as *eis
aiōna aiōnos*) (*ep aiōna kai eti, in sæculum et ultra,* 'forever
and beyond!') are in our version rendered 'forever,' or
'forever and ever'; but so far from necessarily implying endlessness, they are used of many Jewish ordinances which
ceased centuries ago, such as the sprinkling of the lintel at the
Passover (Ex. xii: 24); the Aaronic priesthood and its institu-
tions (Ex. xxix: 9, xl: 15; Lev. iii: 17; Numb. xviii: 19); the
inheritance given to Caleb (Josh. xiv: 9); Solomon's temple
(I. Kings viii: 13); the period of a slave's life (Deut. xv: 17;
Job xli: 4); the burning of the fire upon the altar ('The fire
shall ever be burning upon the altar; it shall never go out,'
Lev. vi: 13, etc.); and the leprosy of Gehazi (II. Kings v: 27)·
How purely figurative these phrases are, may be seen by such
passages as the following:—'The land thereof shall become
burning pitch: it shall not be quenched night or day;
the smoke thereof shall go up forever' (Isa. xxxiv:
10). And so fully is this a recognized idiom that in Deut.
xxiii: 3, 6, we find 'forever' put side by side with 'till
the tenth generation;' and though it is added 'thou shalt not

---

[22] Excursus in Eternal Hope.

seek their peace and prosperity forever,' yet of the very Moabites and Ammonites, of whom this is spoken, we find a prophecy of peace and comfort in Jer. xlviii: 47, xlix: 6. That the adjective *aiōnios* is applied to some things which are 'endless' does not, of course, for one moment prove that the word itself meant 'endless,' and to introduce this rendering into many passages would be utterly impossible and absurd. To translate it in a few passages by 'everlasting,' when in the large majority of passages it is rendered 'eternal,' is a purely wanton and arbitrary variation, which unhappily occurs in one and the same verse (Matt. xxv: 46)."

Let us now illustrate the usage of the word connected with punishment. Ps. ix: 5, "Thou *hast* destroyed the wicked." How? The explanation follows, "Thou hast *put out their name forever and ever.*"[23] This is not endless torment, but oblivion. Solomon elsewhere observes, Prov. x: 7, "The name of the wicked shall rot," while David says, Ps. cxii: 6, " The righteous shall be in *everlasting* remembrance.' Ps. lxxviii: 66, "He put them (his enemies) to a *perpetual* reproach." Isa. xxxiii: 14, " Who among us shall dwell with the devouring fire? Who among us shall dwell with *everlasting* burnings?" The prophet is here speaking of God's temporal judgments represented by fire.' "The earth mourneth; Lebanon is ashamed; the people shall be as the burnings of lime." Who will dwell in safety amid these fiery judgments,—these aionian burnings? "He that walks uprightly." Earthly judgments among which the upright are to dwell in safety are here described, and not endless fire hereafter. Jer. xvii: 4, "Ye have kindled a fire in mine anger which shall burn *forever.*" Where was this to be? The preceding verse informs us. "I will cause thee to serve thine enemies in a land which thou knowest not." Jer. xxiii: 40, "I will bring an *everlasting* reproach upon you; and a *perpetual* shame which shall not be forgotten." The connection fully explains this; verse 39,—"I will utterly forget you, and I will forsake you, and the city

---

[23] τὸν αἰῶνα καὶ εἰς τὸν αἰῶνα τοῦ αἰῶνος.

6

that I gave you and your fathers." See Jer. xx: 11. Mal. i: 4, "The people against whom the Lord hath indignation *forever*." This is an announcement of God's judgment on Edom: "They shall build but I will throw down; and they shall call them the border of wickedness, and the people against whom the Lord hath indignation forever."

Dan. xii: 2, "And many of them that sleep in the dust of the earth shall awake, some to *everlasting* life, and some to shame and *everlasting* contempt." When was this to take place? "At that time." What time? Verse 31, chap. xi, speaks of the coming of "the abomination that maketh desolate." Jesus says, (Matt. xxiv: 15, 16; Luke xxi: 20, 21,) "When ye, therefore (the disciples), shall see the abomination of desola-tion, spoken of by Daniel the prophet, stand in the holy place, then let them which be in Judea flee to the mountains. And when ye shall see Jerusalem compassed with armies, then know that the desolation thereof is nigh. Then let them which are in Judea flee to the mountains; and let them which are in the midst of it depart out; and let not them that are in the countries enter thereinto." Daniel says this was to be (xii: 7), "When he shall have accomplished to scatter the power of the holy people." And he says, "At that time there shall be a time of trouble, such as there never was since there was a nation, even to that same time." Jesus says, "For then shall be great tribulation, such as was not since the beginning of the world to this time; no, nor ever shall be." And Jesus tells us when that was, "This generation shall not pass away till all these things be fulfilled." The events described in Daniel are the same as those in Matt. xxiv, and came in this world, in the generation that crucified Jesus.

The phrase, "sleeping in the dust of the earth," is of course employed above figuratively, to indicate sloth, spiritual lethargy, as in Ps. xliv: 25; Isa. xxv: 12, xxvi: 5; I. Tim. v: 6. Rev. iii: 1, "For our soul is bowed down to the dust." "And the fortress of the high fort of thy walls shall he bring down, lay low, and bring to the ground, even to the dust." "For he bringeth down them that dwell on high; the lofty city, he layeth it low; he layeth it low even to the ground; he bringeth it even to the dust." "But she that liveth in pleasure is dead while she liveth." "I know thy works; that thou hast a name, and that thou livest and art dead." It was a prophecy of the moral awakening that came at the advent of Jesus, and was then fulfilled. When we come to Matt. xxiv and xxv we shall see the nature of this judgment. Balfour describes it,[24] "They" (those who obeyed the call of Jesus), "heard the voice of the Son of God, and lived. (See John v: 21, 25, 28, 29; Eph. v: 14.) The rest kept on till the wrath of God came on them to the uttermost. They all, at last, awoke; but it was to shame and everlasting contempt, in being dispersed among all nations, and they have become a by-word and an hissing even unto this day. Jeremiah, in chapter xxiii: 39, 40, predicted this very punishment and calls it an 'everlasting reproach and a perpetual shame.'"

These few passages, not one of which conveys a hint of endless punishment, are all that connect our word with punishment in the Old Testament.

Prof. S. C. Bartlett, D. D., of Dartmouth College, declares that the intrinsic meaning of the word rendered everlasting in the Old Testament is endless duration. He says:[25]—"Universalists make much parade of a few instances in which the Hebrew term for 'everlasting' denotes something less than absolute eternity, as 'the everlasting hills.' But the phrase, when applied to future time, *always denotes the longest duration of which its subject is capable.* 'Everlasting hills' are those which will continue to the end of the world. 'He shall serve thee forever,' *i. e.,* during the longest period of which he is capable,—his whole life. Hannah devoted Samuel to the Lord 'forever,' (I. Sam. i: 22); *i. e.,* he was never to return to private life. 'An ordinance forever,' is one which lasts through the whole dispensation of which it is a part.

---

[24] Second Inquiry.   [25] Modern Universalism, p. 82.

Such cases, few in number, do not contravene in spirit the scores of instances in which it signifies absolute eternity, the original and proper sense of the term."

Now, 1. If absolute eternity were the meaning of the word, it is only used in its true sense when applied to God, for "absolute eternity" is without beginning as well as without end, and can only belong to God.

2. It is used with limited duration in the great majority of cases in the Bible, as we show specifically.

3. It is not generally used to mean "the longest duration of which its subject is capable." Take the "everlasting hills" referred to by Dr. Bartlett,—every one of them is in process of destruction, and will one day be destroyed, before the earth shall be; for "every valley shall be exalted, and every mountain and hill shall be made low," Isa. xl: 4. Besides, the term is applied in the Bible to hills that had already been destroyed! Hab. iii: 6, "The everlasting hills were scattered." So of another passage quoted by Dr. Bartlett,—"He shall serve thee forever." It was not to be during the whole life, but on the recurrence of the year of jubilee the service expired by a statute of limitation, with which Dr. Bartlett should be familiar. This demonstrates the error of his dictum that when the word does not mean "absolute eternity," it means as long as the duration of the dispensation of which it is a part.

4. He begs the whole question, by asserting the thing to be proved. Suppose punishment were to last "as long as the dispensation of which it is a part," the main question will return, How long is that,—what is that dispensation? What is it that punishment is inflicted for? When we answer, *Sin*, we meet Dr. Bartlett on his own ground, and annihilate him with his own sword, turned upon himself. When we consider sin as the act of a finite being, and punishment as the act of a merciful Father, to eradicate sin, æonian punishment must, from the nature of things, be limited. God's child is sin-sick. Will the wise and good Physician-father physic the patient for ever, or cure him? It is necessary for Dr. Bartlett to prove that the punishment of the Father is in its nature and necessa-

rily endless, before he can apply his own false definition to the word.

Thus this author manages in one brief paragraph to be false in his alleged statement of facts; false in his application even of his own false statements; false in his exegesis, and thoroughly erroneous throughout.

If endless punishment awaits millions of the human race, and if it is denoted by this word, how could it be possible that only David, Isaiah, Jeremiah, Daniel, and Malachi should use it to define the duration of punishment, less than a dozen times, while Job, Moses, Joshua, Ruth, Ezra, Nehemiah, Esther, Solomon, Ezekiel, Hosea, Joel, Amos, Obadiah, Jonah, Micah, Nahum, Habakkuk, Zephaniah, Haggai, and Zachariah never employ it thus? Such reticence would be criminal, on the popular hypothesis. These holy men should and would have made every sentence bristle with the word, and thus have borne the awful message to the soul with an emphasis that could be neither resisted nor disputed. The fact that it is so seldom, and by so few, applied to punishment, and never in the Old Testament to punishment beyond death, demonstrates that it cannot mean endless.

The best critics concede that the doctrine of endless punishment is not taught in the Old Testament. But the word in dispute is found in connection with punishment in the Old Testament. This is a concession on their part that the word has no such meaning in the Old Testament, as endless duration. Milman:—"The lawgiver (Moses) maintains a profound silence on that fundamental article, if not of political, at least of religious, legislation—rewards and punishments of another life." Warburton:—"In no one place of the Mosaic institutes is there the least mention of the rewards and punishments of another life." Paley, Jahn, and Whateley are to the same purport, and H. W. Beecher says, "If we had only the Old Testament we could not tell if there were any future punishment." [26]

Nothing can be more certain than that the general meaning of all forms of the word in the Old Testament is limited duration.

Four questions here press the mind with irresistible force, and they can receive only one answer. 1. Had God intended endless punishment, would the Old Testament have failed to reveal it clearly, unmistakably? 2. If God does not announce it in the Old Testament, is it supposable that he has revealed it elsewhere? 3. Would he for thousands of years conceal so awful a destiny from millions whom he had created and exposed to it? 4. If not in the Old Testament, among the severe penalties of the law, ought we to expect to find it in the milder messages of Gospel grace? No Christian ought to be willing to impeach his Heavenly Father by withholding an indignant negative to these questions.

USAGE.—III.—*JEWISH GREEK.*

Unfortunately but very little Jewish-Greek literature, contemporary with Christ and his apostles, survives. The targums are of dates long subsequent to the Christian era, so that they can throw little light on the meaning of words among the Greek-speaking Jews at the time of Christ. By contact with the heathen, and from other causes, they had greatly degen-

---

[26] Hist. Jews, Vol. II., p. 117; Div. Leg., Vol. III., pp. 1-2, Vol. V.; Sermon XIII. Archæology, p. 398; Essays, p 44. Christian Union.

erated in their religious ideas, and the traditions and fables contained in the targums are of slight value in the discussion of the great question of man's destiny.

But of the Jews who were contemporary with Christ we may safely make one assertion: they used the word under consideration precisely as it was used in the Old Testament. They were diligent students of the Septuagint, and they could put no construction on our word different from that which we have seen it to carry in the Greek Scriptures, with which they were perfectly familiar.

We find the truth of this statement established as we consult Josephus, who applies the word to the imprisonment to which John, the tyrant, was condemned by the Romans; to the reputation of Herod; to the memorial erected in re-building the temple, already destroyed when he wrote; to the worship in the temple, which, in the same sentence, he says was destroyed; to the glory acquired by soldiers, and he styles the time between the promulgation of the law and his writing, a long *aiōn*.[1] To accuse him of attaching any other meaning than that of indefinite duration to the word, is to accuse him of stultifying himself. In his treatise on Daniel, he says, "He was held in the greatest favor and honor by kings and people, whilst he lived; and, having died, he is still held in (μνήμην αἰώνιον) eternal remembrance." In his work against Apion, "It is plain from this fact, how much faith we have in these writings; for no one has dared, so long a time having already passed away (τοσοίτον αἰῶνος ἤδη παρῳχηκότος), to add anything, nor to diminish, nor to change anything."

---

[1] The way in which Josephus uses the word can be seen in the following instances of its application to temporal affairs. He speaks of the fame of an army as "a happy life, and æonian glory." Ant. Jud., Lib. IV., Cap. 6, § 5, εὐδαίμονα βίον καὶ κλέος αἰώνιον παμισχεῖν, etc.,—*et gloria donet immortali.* He calls a memorial æonian,—Ant. Jud., Lib. I., C. 13, § 4, καὶ μνήμην αἰώνιον —*in sempiterna memoria.* Ant. Jud., Lib. XII., C. 7, § 3, αἰώνιον τὴν εὐκλειαν etc.,—*vos æternam manere gloriam,* etc. Ant. Jud., Lib. XV., C. 11, § 1, καὶ πρὸς αἰώνιον μνήμην ἀσκέσειν,—*atque futurum ad sempiternam.* See also ib., Lib. IV., C. 6, § 5; Lib. XV., C. 15, § 5; De Bello, Lib. VI., C. 2, § 1; C. 9, § 4.

But when he wishes to describe endless duration he employs other and unequivocal terms. Of the doctrine of the Pharisees. he says,[2] "They believe that spirits possess a deathless vigor, and that under the earth there will be rewards and punishments, as they have lived virtuously or wickedly in this life, and that these last are to be kept in an eternal imprisonment (*eirgmon aïdion*), etc."

Again,[3] "Of the two first named, the Pharisees are regarded as most skilful in interpreting their laws, and constitute the first sect. They ascribe everything to fate and to God, but allow that to do what is right is mainly within the power of men, though fate always coöperates. All souls are incorruptible, but while those of good men are removed into other bodies, those of bad men are subject to eternal punishment, (*aïdios timoria*)."

Elsewhere he says that the Essenes "Allot to bad souls a dark, tempestuous place, full of never-ceasing punishment (*timoria adialeipton*), where they suffer a deathless punishment (*athanaton timorian*)." It is true that he sometimes applies *aiōnion* to punishment, but this is not his usual custom, and he seems to have done this as one might use the word great to denote eternal duration, that is, an indefinite term to describe infinity. But *aïdion* and *athanaton* are his favorite terms. These are unequivocal. Were only *aiōnion* used to define the Jewish idea of the duration of future punishment, we should have no proof that it was supposed by them to be endless.

---

[2] Ant. Jud., Lib. XVIII., C. 1, § 3, Ἀθάνατόν τε ἰσχὺν ταῖς ψυχαῖς πίστις αὐτοῖς εἶναι, καὶ ὑπὸ χθονὸς δικαιώσεις τε καὶ τιμὰς οἷς ἀρετῆς ἢ κακίας ἐπιτήδευσις ἐν τῷ βίῳ γέγονε, καὶ ταῖς μὲν εἰργμὸν ἀίδιον, etc.

[3] De Bello Jud., B. II., C. 8, § 14, Δύο δὲ προτέρον φαρισαίοι μὲν, οἱ δοκοῦντες μετὰ ἀκριβείας ἐξηγεῖσθαι τὰ νόμιμα καὶ τὴν πρώτην ἐπάγοντες αἵρεσιν, εἱμαρμένῃ τε καὶ Θεῷ προσάπτουσι πάντα, καὶ τὸ μὲν πράττειν τὰ δίκαια καὶ μὴ, κατὰ τὸ πλεῖστον ἐπὶ τοῖς ἀνθρώποις κεῖσθαι, βοηθεῖν δὲ εἰς ἕκαστον καὶ τὴν εἱμαρμένην· ψυχὴν δὲ πᾶσαν μὲν ἄφθαρτον, μεταβαίνειν δὲ εἰς ἕτερον σῶμα τὴν τῶν ἀγαθῶν μόνην, τὴν δὲ τῶν φαύλων ἀιδίῳ τιμωρίᾳ κολάζεσθαι.

Philo, who was contemporary with Christ, generally used *aïdion* to denote endless, and *aiōnion* to describe temporary duration. Dr. Mangey, in his edition of Philo, says he never used *aiōnion* for interminable duration. He uses the exact phraseology of Matthew xxv: 46, precisely as Christ used it. "It is better not to promise than not to give prompt assistance, for no blame follows in the former case, but in the latter there is dissatisfaction from the weaker class, and a deep hatred and everlasting punishment[4] from such as are more powerful."[5] Here we have the precise terms employed by our Lord, which show that *aiōnion* did not mean endless, but did mean limited duration, in the time of Christ. Speaking of the solicitude of the brute for its offspring, he observes,[6] "Perceiving from afar with a long-reaching (*aiōnia*) sagacity." Philo adopts *athanaton, ateleuteton,* or *aïdion,* to denote endless, and *aiōnion* for temporary duration. In one place occurs this sentence concerning the wicked,[7] ζῆν ἀποθνήσκοντα ἀεὶ καὶ τρόπον τινὰ θάνατον αθάνατον ὑπομείνων καὶ ἀτελεὶτητον, "to live always dying, and to undergo, as it were, an immortal and interminable death."

Stephens, in his Thesaurus, quotes from a Jewish work,[8]— "These they called *aiōnios,* hearing that they had performed the sacred rites for three entire generations."[9] This shows conclusively that the expression "three generations" was then one full equivalent of *aiōnion.*

Now, these eminent scholars were Jews who wrote in Greek, and who certainly knew the meaning of the words they employed, and they give to the æonian words the meaning

---

[4] κολασις αἰώνιος.

[5] Fragmenta, Tom. II., p. 667, ed. Mangey, 1741.

[6] De Humanitate, Tom. II., pp. 396-7.

[7] De Præmiis and Pœnis, Tom. II., pp. 19-20, Mangey's ed.

[8] Solom. Parab.

[9] Beecher, Hist. Fut. Ret., pp. 73-75. Dollinger, quoted by Beecher. Philo was born twenty-five years before Christ, and was learned in Greek philosophy,—especially reverenced Plato. His use of Greek words would be perfectly accurate, and is of the highest authority.

that we are contending for,—indefinite duration, to be determined by the subject treated.

Thus the Jews of our Savior's time avoided using the word *aiŏnion* to denote endless duration, for, applied all through the Bible to temporary affairs, it would not teach it. If he had intended to inculcate the doctrine held by the Jews, Jesus would certainly have used their terms. But he threatened age-lasting, or long-enduring discipline to the believers in endless punishment. *Aiŏnion* was his word, while theirs was *aïdion, adialeipton,* or *athanaton.* He thus rejected their doctrines, by not only not employing their phraseology, but by using only those words connected with punishment that denote limited duration.

It is sometimes said that Jesus adopted the phraseology current at the time he spoke, and used by others to convey the idea of interminable torment; but we have now shown that he did nothing of the kind. Instead of *thanaton athanaton,* immortal death; *eirgmon aïdion,* eternal imprisonment; *aïdion timorian,* eternal torment, and *thanaton ateleuteton,* interminable death, he used *aiŏnion kolasin,* the adjective denoting limited duration, and the noun suffering, issuing in amendment.[10] Not only did he refuse to indorse the views of the Jews, acquired from the heathen, but he absolutely condemned them. Referring to the cruel men who procured his death, Jesus said to his disciples,[11] "Take heed and beware of the leaven (doctrine) of the Pharisees and the Sadducees" (believers in endless misery and believers in destruction). Had *aiŏnion* been the strongest word, especially had it unequivocally denoted endless duration, who does not see that it would have been in general use as applied to punishment by the Jewish Greeks, of nineteen centuries ago, who believed in endless punishment, but who stated it in stronger words than the æonian phraseology?

---

[10] For an exposition of *kolasin,* rendered punishment in Matt. **xxv: 46,** see next chapter.

[11] Matt. xvi: 6.

Now, does not the fact that the Jewish Greeks contemporary with Christ generally used other words, and those that are stronger, as we shall show when we come to treat the New Testament usage, when they defined that endless punishment in which they were believers, and employed æonian words to describe temporary duration, demonstrate that the æonian words did not then denote endless duration? And if such was not their meaning then, is it not preposterous to suppose that Jesus gave to them such a meaning—one that no one else had ever given them, and one that no one would understand them to signify?

We thus have an unbroken chain of Lexicography, and Classic, Old Testament, and Contemporaneous Usage, all allowing to the word the meaning we claim for it, so that we are compelled, as we open the New Testament, to expect to find it employing the æonian terms in the sense of limited duration.

USAGE.—IV.—*THE NEW TESTAMENT.*

Nothing can be more evident than that Jesus and his Apostles used all words in exactly the sense they had in the Old Testament. To give words that were found in the Old Testament new meanings, with no intimation of a change, would be to mislead those who should hear or read them. Such a course should be insupposable. Instead of being quoted from the Hebrew Bible, more than five-sixths of the Old Testament passages in the New Testament are directly from the LXX. The Septuagint was the Bible referred to by Christ and the Apostles. The word whose biography we are

writing, therefore, must have the same meaning in the New
Testament as in the LXX. This we have seen to be indefinite
duration. An examination of the New Testament will show
that the meaning is the same as in the Old Testament.

The different forms of the word occur in the New Testament one hundred and ninety-nine times; the noun one hundred and twenty-eight, and the adjective seventy-one times. In
the Established Version the noun is rendered seventy-two times
ever, twice *eternal*, thirty-six times *world*, seven times *never*,
three times *evermore*, twice *worlds*, twice *ages*, once *course*,
once *world without end*, and twice it is passed over without
any word affixed as a translation of it. The adjective is rendered once *ever*, forty-two times *eternal*, three times *world*,
twenty-five times *everlasting*, and once *former ages*.

1. It is ten times applied to the kingdom of Christ. Luke
i: 33, 35, "And he shall reign over the house of Jacob *forever*;
and of his kingdom there shall be no end. As he spake to our
fathers, to Abraham, and to his seed *forever*," (that is,
anciently). Heb. vi: 20, "Whither the forerunner is for us
entered, even Jesus, made a high priest *forever* after the
order of Melchisedec." "For he testifieth (vii: 17, 21), Thou
art a priest *forever* after the order of Melchisedec." II. Pet. i:
11, "For so an entrance shall be ministered unto you abundantly into the *everlasting* kingdom of our Lord and Savior
Jesus Christ." (II. Pet. iii: 18 may mean endless duration,
as may Rev. i: 6, and I. Pet. iv: 11). Rev. xi: 15, "And
the seventh angel sounded; and there were great voices in
heaven, saying, The kingdoms of this world are become the
kingdoms of our Lord, and of his Christ; and he shall reign
forever and ever." But the passages that declare that Christ's
kingdom is an everlasting kingdom, and that he is to reign forever, must denote limited duration, for the reason that the
kingdom of Christ is to end, and his reign cease, when he shall
have delivered up the kingdom to the Father, as in I. Cor. xv:
24, 25, "Then cometh the end, when he shall have delivered
up the kingdom to God, even the Father; when he shall have
put down all rule, and all authority and power. For he must

reign, till he hath put all enemies under his feet." His reign is limited to the period when he shall have subdued all souls to God, and then the Son will be subject to the Father. So that a limited duration is taught in all the passages that call the reign of Christ *everlasting, forever,* etc. Kindred to this is Rev. xiv: 6, "The *everlasting* gospel." The gospel is good news. When all shall have learned its truths it will no longer be news. There will be no such thing as gospel extant. Faith will be fruition, hope lost in sight, and the *aiōnion* gospel, like the *aiōnion* covenant of the elder dispensation, will be abrogated, not destroyed.

2. It is applied to the Jewish age more than thirty times: I. Cor. x: 11, "Now all these things happened unto them for ensamples; and they are written for our admonition, upon whom the *ends of the world* are come." Matt. xii: 32, "And whosoever speaketh a word against the Son of man, it shall be forgiven him; but whosoever speaketh against the Holy Ghost, it shall not be forgiven him, neither in this *world*, neither in the world to come." Xiii: 22, 39, 40, 49, "He also that received seed among the thorns is he that heareth the word; and the care of this *world*, and the deceitfulness of riches, choke the word, and he becometh unfruitful. The enemy that sowed them is the devil; the harvest is the end of the *world*, and the reapers are the angels. As, therefore, the tares are gathered and burned in the fire: so shall it be in the end of this *world*. So shall it be at the end of the *world*; the angels shall come forth, and sever the wicked from among the just." Xxiv: 3, "What shall be the sign of thy coming and of the end of the *world?*" Xxviii: 20, "Teaching them to observe all things whatsoever I have commanded you: and, lo, I am with you alway, even unto the end of the *world.*" Mark iv: 19, "And the cares of this *world*, and the deceitfulness of riches, and the lusts of other things entering in, choke the word, and it becometh unfruitful." Consult also Luke i: 70, xvi: 8, xx: 34; John ix: 32; Acts iii: 21, xv: 18; Rom. xii: 2; I. Cor. ii: 6, 7, 8, iii: 18; II. Cor. iv: 4; Gal. i: 4; Eph. i: 21, ii: 2, iii: 9; II.

Tim. iv: 10; Titus ii: 12; Heb. ix: 26. The last citation above exemplifies the use, "But now once in the end of the *world* hath he appeared to put away sin by the sacrifice of himself." The world here referred to is *aiŏn*, and its manifest meaning is the Jewish age. But that ended with the establishment of the kingdom of Christ. So that the word signifies limited duration in all these passages.

3. It is used in the plural in Eph. iii: 21, "The *age* of the *ages*," *tou aiŏnos tŏn aiŏnŏn.* Heb. i: 2, xi: 3, "By whom he made the *worlds*. The *worlds* were framed by the word of God." There can be but one eternity. To say, "By whom he made the eternities," would be to talk nonsense. Endless duration is not inculcated in these texts.

4. The word clearly teaches finite duration in such passages as Rom. xvi: 25; II. Cor. iv: 17; II. Tim. i: 9; Philemon 15; Titus i: 2. Read Rom. xvi: 25, "Since the *world* began." II. Cor. iv: 17, "A far more exceeding and *eternal* weight of glory." Here "and" is a word supplied by the translators, and the literal is "an excessively exceeding æonian weight." But endless cannot be exceeded. Therefore *aiŏnion* does not here mean eternal.

5. The word is used as equivalent to *not* or a *long time*, in Matt. xxi: 19; Mark xi: 14; John xiii: 8; I. Cor. viii: 13. "Peter said unto him 'Thou shalt *never* wash my feet,'" is a specimen of this use of the word.

6. It is applied to life, "everlasting and eternal life." But this phrase does not so much denote the duration, as the quality of the blessed life. It seems to have the sense of durable, rather than endless, in these passages: Matt. xix: 16, 29, xxv: 46; Mark x: 17, 30; Luke x: 25, xvi: 9, xviii: 18, 30; John iii: 15, 16, 36, iv: 14, 36, v: 24, 39, vi: 27, 40, 47, 54, 68, x: 28, xii: 25, 50, xvii: 2, 3; Rom. ii: 7, v: 21, vi: 22, 23; Gal. vi: 8; II. Thess. ii: 16; I. Tim. i: 16, vi: 12; Titus i: 2, iii: 7; Heb. v: 9; I. John i: 2, ii: 25, iii: 15, v: 11, 13, 20; Jude 21; Mark x: 30; Luke xviii: 30; John iv: 14, vi: 51, 58, viii: 51, 52, x: 28, xi: 26. See this subject treated further on, when it will be

fully shown that "everlasting life" is not the immortal existence hereafter, but the life of faith here or hereafter, regardless of its duration.

7. It is applied to God, Christ, the Gospel, the good, the resurrection world, etc., in which the sense of endless is allowable because imputed to the word by the subject treated, as declared by Schleusner, on pages 33-37 of this book. See Rom. i: 25, ix: 5, xi: 36, xvi: 27; Gal. i: 5; Phil. iv: 20; I. Tim. i: 17; II. Tim. iv: 18; I. John ii: 17; I. Peter v: 11; Rev. vii: 12, xv: 7; Rom. xvi: 26; II. Cor. iv: 18, v: 1; II. Tim. ii. 10; Hebrews vi: 2; ix: 12, 14, 15, xiii: 20; I. Peter v: 10; John viii: 35, xii: 34, xiv: 16; II. Corinthians ix: 9, xi: 31; Ephesians iii: 11; Hebrews vii: 24, 28, xiii: 8, 21; I. Peter i: 25; II. Peter iii: 18; II. John 2; Jude 25; Rev. i: 18, iv: 9, 10, v: 13, x: 6, xxii: 5. The sense of endless is permissible in these passages, just as the word great would acquire a meaning when attached to these subjects, that it would not ordinarily possess.

By considering several passages it will be seen that the word cannot have the sense of endless. Matt. xiii: 22, "The care of this *world*, and the deceitfulness of riches, choke the word," the cares of that age or "time." Verses 39, 40, 49, "The harvest is the end of the world," *i. e.*, age, Jewish age. The same as taught in Matt. xxiv, which some who heard Jesus speak were to live to see, and did see. Luke i: 33, "And he (Jesus) shall reign over the house of Jacob *forever*, and of his kingdom there shall be no end." The meaning is, he shall reign to the ages (*eis tous aiōnas*). That long, indefinite duration is meant here but limited, is evident from I. Cor. xv: 28, "And when all things shall be subdued unto him, then shall the Son also himself be subject unto him that put all things under him, that God may be all in all." His reign is forever, *i. e.*, to the ages, but it is to cease. Luke i: 55, "As he spake to our fathers, to Abraham and to his seed *forever*, (*eōs aiōnos*) that is, anciently. Luke i: 70, "As he spake by the mouth of his holy prophets, which have been since the *world* began," or "from of old," (*ap aiōnos*). Luke xvi: 8,

"For the children of this *world* are in their generation wiser than the children of light." That is, the people of that time were more prudent in the management of their affairs than were the Christians of that day in their plans. John ix: 32, "Since the *world* began was it not heard that any man opened the eyes of one that was born blind." From the age (*ek tou aiōnos*), that is, from the beginning of our knowledge and history. Rom. xvi: 25, "Since the world began," clearly shows a duration less than eternity, inasmuch as the mystery that had been secret since the world began, was then revealed. The mystery was *aiōnion* but did not last eternally. It was "now made manifest" "to all nations." Phil. iv: 20, "Now unto God and our Father be glory *forever and ever,*" for the ages of the ages (*eis tous aiōnas tōn aiōnōn*). (Gal. i: 5, same.) "For the eternities of the eternities," is an absurd expression. But ages of ages is proper. Eternity may be meant here, but if the word *aiōn* expressed the idea, such a reduplication would be weak and improper. I. Tim. vi: 17, "Charge them that are rich in this *world*" (age or time). I. Tim. i: 17, "Now to the King *eternal* (of the ages) be glory for the *ages of the ages.*" What is this but an ascription to the God of the ages? Eternity can only be meant here, as ages on ages imply long, and possibly endless duration. "All the ages are God's; him let the ages glorify," is the full import of the words. Translate the words eternity, and what nonsense: Now to the God of eternities be glory for the eternities of the eternities. Heb. i: 8, "The *age of the age.*" Eph. ii: 7, "That in the *ages* (*aiōns*) to come he might show the exceeding riches of his grace." Here at least two *aiōns* are to come. Certainly one of them must end before the other begins. Eph. iii: 21, "The generations of *the age of the ages.*" II. Tim. iv: 18, "*The ages of the ages.*" The same form of expression is in Heb. xiii: 21; I. Peter iv. 11; Rev. i: 6, iv: 9, v: 13, vii: 12, xiv: 11, xv: 7, xx: 10. When we read that the smoke of torment ascends (*eis tous aiōnas tōn aiōnōn*) for ages of ages, we get the idea of long, but limited duration; for as an age is limited, any number, however great, must be limited. The moment we say the smoke of their torment goes up for eternities of eternities, we transform the sacred rhetoric into jargon. There is but one eternity; therefore, as we read of more than one *aiōn*, it follows that *aiōn* cannot mean eternity. Again, I. Cor. x: 11, "Our admonition, on whom *the ends* of the *aiōns* (ages, *ta tele tōn aiōnōn*) have come." That is, the close of the Mosaic and the beginning of the Gospel age. How absurd to say "ends of the eternities"! Here the apostle had passed more than one, and entered, consequently, upon at least a third, *aiōn*. Heb. ix: 26, "Now at an end of the *ages*." Matt. xiii: 39, 40, xxiv: 4, "The conclusion of the *age*." Eternity has no end, and to say end of eternity is to talk nonsense. II. Tim. i: 9, "Before the *world* began," *i. e.*, before the *aiōnion* times began. There was no beginning to eternity, therefore the adjective *aiōnion* here has no such meaning as eternal. The fact that *aiōn* is said to end and begin, is a demonstration that it does not mean eternity.

Translate the word eternity in most of these passages and how absurd the Bible becomes! Gal. i: 5, "To whom be the glory during the *eternities*, even to the *eternities*." I. Cor. x: 11, "Now all these things happened unto them, for ensamples, and they are written for our admonition upon whom the ends of the *eternities* are come." Eph. ii: 7, "That in the *eternities* coming he might show the exceeding riches of his grace." Col. i: 26, "The mystery which hath been hid from the *eternities* and from the *generations*." Heb. ix: 26, "But now once in the end of the *eternities*, hath he appeared to put away sin by the sacrifice of himself." Matt. xiii: 39, "The harvest is the end of the *eternity*." Matt. xiii: 40, "So shall it be in the end of this *eternity*." Matt. xxiv: 4, "Tell us when shall these things be, and what the sign of thy coming, and of the end of the eternity." But substitute "age" or "ages," and the sense of the Record is preserved. It will be seen that if eternity is the English equivalent of *aiōn*, then we ought to read "this eternity," "that *eternity*," "since the eternity began," "from the beginning of the eternity," "while the eternity standeth," "in the eternities to come," "in the end of the

7

eternity," "a mystery hid from eternities," "eternity and eternity," and all manner of expressions that are unrhetorical, ungrammatical and utterly absurd.

John R. Beard, D. D., author of "Bible Dictionary," Manchester, Eng., thus writes:—"For one moment let us dwell on that word—the word 'everlasting,' or 'eternal.' Now, in the first place, the readers of the English Bible have not to do with that word itself, but with a translation of it. Are the two identical in meaning? Do they each cover the same ground? Certainly not. Our conception of eternity is much more absolute than that of either the Greeks or the Hebrews, with whom the corresponding words denoted generally an indefinite and unknown period. Can we speak of eternities? They could. Yea, 'eternities of eternities,' 'before the eternities,' and 'to the eternities of eternities,' are the forms of speech employed in the New Testament. What then? There are several eternities, and eternities are appended to eternities. Clearly the Greek original signifies much less than its English representative; and if anything less than endless, the word expresses time, and not what we call eternity. Then, the word is also used of subjects which in their nature are of limited duration. It is used of things. Is a thing imperishable or perishable? It is used of this world; but this world passeth away. It is used of times; times, however, can be nothing more than repeated years, days, and hours. It is used of fire; but unquenchable fire is an impossibility, unless fire, which, consuming other things, consumes itself, shares God's deathlessness. It is used of punishment; but the punishment which does not end in reformation is vindictiveness, which cannot be ascribed to the merciful Father, whose name and whose essence is love."

We read in the New Testament of the *beginning* of *aiōn*. The beginning of *aiōn* is spoken of in Luke i: 70 (ἀπ' αἰῶνος), of old, or anciently; John ix: 32 (ἐκ τοῦ αἰῶνος), from the memory of man; Acts iii: 21, and xv: 18 (ἀπ' αἰῶνος), of old, anciently; Eph. iii: 9 (ἀπὸ τῶν αἰώνων), from the ages, of the old dispensation.

There are many *repetitions of aiōn*. The word is repeated in the following passages, to express very great duration: Rev. i: 18, "And behold, I am alive (εἰς τοὺς αἰῶνας τῶν αἰώνων), for ages of ages." Eph. iii: 21 (εἰς πάσας τὰς γενεὰς τοῦ αἰῶνος τῶν αἰώνων), literally, according to Macknight, "through all the eras of the age of ages." I. Tim. i: 17, "To the king of ages (τῶν αἰώνων), the immortal, the incorruptible, and the God only wise, be glory and honor for ages of ages (εἰς τοὺς αἰῶνας τῶν αἰώνων)." Rev. xiv: 11, "The smoke of their torment goeth up (εἰς αἰῶνας αἰώνων) for ages and ages." Sir Isaac Newton says,[1] "The ascending up of the smoke of any burning thing *forever and ever*, is put for the continuation of a conquered people under the misery of perpetual subjection and slavery." See Gal. i: 5; Phil. iv: 20; II. Tim. iv: 18; Heb. i: 8, and xiii: 21; I. Peter iv: 11, and v: 11; Rev. iv: 9, 10, and v: 13, 14, and vii: 12, and x: 6, and xi: 15, and xv: 7, and xix: 3, and xx: 10, and xxii: 5.

It means *more than eternal*. If *aiōn* signifies eternity, and *aiōnios* eternal, then there is nothing *more*, or *beyond* eternity, or eternal. But the apostle (II. Cor. iv: 17) uses the remarkable phrase (καθ' ὑπερβολὴν εἰς ὑπερβολὴν αἰώνιον βάρος δόξης), exceeding eternal to an excess. If *aiōn* signifies eternity, then (in Dan. xii: 3) we read, *to eternities, and further* (εἰς τοὺς αἰῶνας καὶ ἔτι). In Ex. xv: 18, "The Lord shall reign (τὸν αἰῶνα καὶ ἐπ' αἰῶνα καὶ ἔτι) from eternity even to eternity, and further." In Micah iv: 5, "We will walk in the name of the Lord our God (εἰς τὸν αἰῶνα καὶ ἐπέκεινα) to eternity and beyond." Dan. vii: 18, "to eternity, even to an eternity of an eternity." Ps. xlviii: 14, "For this God is our God (εἰς τὸν αἰῶνα καί εἰς τὸν αἰῶνα τοῦ αἰῶνος), to an age, and to an age of an age." The phrase, "to an age, and to an age of an age," or, "to eternity, and to an eternity of an eternity," may be found, Ps. cxix: 44, and cxiv: 2, 21, and cxlviii: 6.[2]

It acquires *various meanings*. This is seen in many passages. Luke xx: 34, 35, "The children of this world marry,

---

[1] Prophecies of Daniel and Revelations, London Edition, 1738, p. 18.

[2] This *aiōn*, the *aiōn*, that *aiōn* occur twenty-seven times in the New Testament. This or that *age* is proper, but this or that eternity is not.

and are given in marriage; but they which shall be accounted worthy to obtain that *world*, . . . are equal unto the angels," etc. Here "that world" (*tou aiōnos*) denotes the eternal world, not because the word *intrinsically* means that, but because the resurrection state is the topic of discourse. The words literally mean that age or epoch, but in this instance the immortal world is the subject that defines the word and extends its meaning. So when the word refers to God, it denotes a different duration than when it applies to the Jewish dispensation. That in some of the places referred to the mooted word has the sense of endless, we do not question, but in all such cases it derives that meaning from the subject connected with it.

Aiōn occurs in the New Testament sixty-three times in the singular, eighteen times in the plural, twenty-three times in a reduplicate form,—in all, one hundred and four times.

It is found twenty times "this world," six "the world," once "that world": Matt. xii: 22, 39, 40, 49, xiii: 32, xxiv: 3, xxviii: 20; Mark iv: 19; Luke i: 70, xvi: 8, xx: 34, 35; Acts iii: 21; Rom. xii: 2; I. Cor. i: 20, ii: 6, (twice) 8, iii: 18; II. Cor. iv: 4; Gal. i: 4; Eph. i: 21, ii: 2, vi: 12; I. Tim. vi: 17; II. Tim. iv: 10; Tit. ii: 12.

It is rendered twenty times "forever," seven times "never," three times the "world to come," two "ever," one "since the world began," one "from the beginning of the world," one "while the world standeth," and one time "forevermore." The places are as follows:—Matt. xxi: 19; Mark x: 30, xi: 14; Luke i: 55, xviii: 30; John iv: 14, vi: 51, 58, viii: 35 (twice), 51, 52, ix: 32, x: 28, xi: 26, xii: 34, xiii: 8, xiv: 16; Acts xv: 18; I Cor. viii: 13; II. Cor. ix: 9; Heb. v: 6, vi: 5, 20, vii: 17, 21, 24, 28; I. Pet. i: 23, 25; II. Pet. iii: 18; I. John ii: 17; II. John 2.

It is found eighteen times in the plural form. Three times translated "the world," twice "the worlds," and one time "the ages": I. Cor. ii: 7, x: 11; Eph. ii: 7; Heb. i: 2, ix: 26, xi: 3. It is seven times rendered "forever," twice "eternal," one time "forevermore," one time "from the beginning of the world," and one time "ages":—Matt. vi: 13; Luke i: 33; Rom. i: 25,

ix: 5, xi: 36, xvi: 27; II. Cor. xi: 31; Eph. iii: 9, 11; Col. i: 26;
I. Tim. i: 17; Heb. xiii: 8.

It is in a doubled or reduplicate form twenty-three times:
twenty-one times translated "forever and ever," one time
"forevermore," and one time "throughout all ages, world without end." This phrase is employed ten times to express the
interminable duration of the glory of God, as follows:—Gal. i:
5; Eph. iii: 21; Phil. iv: 20; I. Tim. i: 17; II. Tim. iv: 18;
Heb. xiii: 21; I. Pet. iv: 11, v: 11; Rev. i: 6, vii: 12. It is
four times used to express the eternity of Deity, Rev. iv: 9,
10, x: 6, xv: 7; once to denote the eternity of the throne of
Jehovah, Heb. i: 8; once to express the immortality and
eternity of Christ, Rev. i: 18; once to show the duration of
Christ's reign, Rev. xi: 15; twice to express the duration of his
glory, Rev. v: 13, 14; once to express the duration of the
happiness of the redeemed, Rev. xxii: 5; once the duration of
the punishment of those who had worshiped the beast and his
image, Rev. xiv: 11; once the duration of the fire that shall
burn Babylon, Rev. xix: 3; and once to denote the duration
of the torment which the devil, the beast, and the false
prophet shall endure in the lake of fire, Rev. xx; 10: "Unto the
ages of the ages."

Dr. Whiton[3] observes:—"An examination of all the passages in the New Testament, in which the word occurs, will
yield the following results:—1. That it denotes a period of duration. 2. That it is used very frequently, much more often than
by the Classic Greek, in the plural. This fact is in the way
of the assertion that *æon* has inherently the idea of *infinite*
duration, for only finite things can have the plural. We can
not speak of the coming *eternities*. But Paul speaks (Eph.
ii: 7) of 'the ages (*æons*) to come.' 3. That the present
world-period or course of things, is spoken of *this æon*, or
the æon, or *an æon*. 4. That the period or course of things
which is immediately to succeed the present is likewise called
that æon, or *the æon*, or *the coming æon*. 5. That past

[3] Is Eternal Punishment Endless? pp. 11-13.

duration, the course or courses of things that have precéded the present, is called *the œons*, or simply *œons*. 6. That future duration, in its whole compass, is described as a succession of *œons*. 7. That the regular phrases for unlimited duration,—*for the œons*, or, for the *œons of the œons*, strictly denote an indefinite succession of finite periods or *œons*. 8. *That there is no single word that regularly carries the meaning of our word eternity*."

As day, the noun, possesses daily for its adjective, and month and monthly, year and yearly describe the same duration, whether the noun or adjective be employed, so the noun *aiōn* in Matt. xxiv: 3, must mean the same as *aiōnios* in Matt. xxv: 46. If the one is age or world, the other must be worldly or age-long; better still, *œonian*. Eternal is utterly wrong. Or, if *aiōnion* in Matt. xxv: 46 meant endless, then the disciples must have asked Jesus in Matt. xxiv: 3, "What shall be the sign of the end of eternity!"

A birds-eye view of the way in which the noun is used will serve to prove its limited time-sense. Matt. xxviii: 20, "End of the *œon*." Mark iv: 19, "Cares of the *œon*." Luke i: 33, "Shall reign over the house of Jacob for the *œons*." John iv: 14, "Shall not thirst for the *œon*," E. V., "forever." John ix: 32, "Since the *œon* began." Rom. xii: 2, "Be not conformed to this *œon*." I. Cor. ii: 7, "Before the *œons*." I. Cor. x: 11, "The ends of the *œons* are come." II. Cor. xi: 31, "God blessed for the *œons*." Eph. ii: 2, "According to the course of the *œon*." Eph. ii: 7, "The *œons* to come." Eph. iii: 21, "To all the generations of the *œon* of the *œons*." I. Tim. i: 17, "The king of the *œons*." Heb. i: 2, "He made the *œons*," E. V. "worlds." Rev. iv: 9, "Who liveth to the *œons* of the *œons*," E. V., "forever and ever."

Let us further indicate its varied use. Matt. vi: 13 is probably spurious,[4] "Thine is the glory *forever*," that is, through the ages. Here eternity may be implied, but the phrase "forever" literally means " for the ages." Mark x: 30,

---

[4] Griesbach, Knapp, Wetstein.

"But he shall receive a hundred fold now in this time, houses, and brethren, and sisters, and mothers, and children, and lands, with persecutions; and in the *world* to come *eternal* life," literally, in the age to come, the life of that age, *i. e.*, gospel, spiritual, Christian life. We have shown that the world to come denotes the Christian dispensation. Mark xi: 14, "No man eat fruit of thee hereafter *for ever*," that is, "in the age," meaning the period of the tree's existence. John xii: 34, "The people answered him, We have heard out of the law that Christ abideth *forever*" (to the age). The Jews believed their dispensation was to continue, and that Messiah would remain so long as it would last. This language means that Christ was to remain through the Mosaic epoch. So the Jews thought. John xiii: 8, "Thou shalt *never* wash my feet," is equivalent to "Thou shalt not wash my feet." John xiv: 16, "And I will pray the Father and he shall give you another Comforter, that he may abide with you *for ever*" (*eis ton aiōna*), "unto the age," that is, accompany them into the coming or Christian era. John vi: 51, 58, "If any man eat of this bread he shall live *for ever*" (*eis ton aiōna*), "into the age," that is, enjoy the life of the *æon* that is to come, the Christian life. Its duration is not described here at all. John viii: 35, "And the servant abideth not in the house *for ever* (to the age); but the Son abideth ever." The Jews are here told that their religion is to be superseded by Christ. They are to leave the house because slaves to sin, while the Son will remain permanently. John viii: 51, 52, "Verily, verily, I say unto you, If a man keep my saying, he shall *never* see death. Then said the Jews unto him, Now we know that thou hast a devil. Abraham is dead, and the prophets; and thou sayest, If a man keep my saying he shall *never* taste of death." Moral, spiritual death is impossible to a man so long as he keeps the sayings of Christ, is the full meaning of the words.

The adjective *aiōnios* is (incorrectly) said by Professor Stuart[5] to occur sixty-six times in the New Testament, but we

---

[5] Ex. Essays, p. 46.

make it seventy-two times. Of these, fifty-seven are used in relation to the happiness of the righteous; three in relation to God or his glory; four are of a miscellaneous nature; and seven relate to the subject of punishment. Now, these fifty-seven denote indefinite duration, "everlasting life" being a life that may or may not—certainly does not always—endure forever. Endless duration is allowable, when the subject compels it, but the general usage is otherwise. Of course, the adjective must mean the same as the noun.

Thus, the preponderance of usage in the New Testament is limited duration. But if the preponderance were otherwise, we ought, in order to vindicate God's character, to understand the word in the sense of limited when describing a Father's punishment of his children. But with more than one hundred and fifty out of one hundred and ninety-nine instances limited, we are prepared, regardless of other considerations, and guided only by the use of the word, to understand it as not conveying the force of endlessness when applied to punishment.

In how many instances, in the entire New Testament, does the word in all its forms qualify punishment? Only fourteen times in thirteen passages in the entire New Testament, and these were uttered on ten occasions only! The noun, Matt. xii: 32; Mark iii: 29; II. Peter ii: 17; Jude 13; Rev. xiv: 11, xix: 3, xx: 10. The adjective, Matt. xviii: 8, xxv: 41, 46; Mark iii: 29; II. Thess. i: 9; Jude 7; Heb. vi: 2.

Now, if God's punishments are limited, we can understand how this word should be used only fourteen times to define them. But if they are endless, how can we explain the employment of this equivocal word connected with punishment only fourteen times in the entire New Testament? A doctrine that, if true, ought to crowd every sentence, frown in every line, only stated fourteen times, and that, too, by a word whose uniform meaning everywhere else is limited duration! The idea is preposterous, incredible. If the word denote limited duration, the punishments threatened in the New Testament are like those that experience teaches follow transgression.

But if it mean endless, how can we account for the fact that neither Luke nor John records one instance of its use by the Savior, and Matthew but four, and Mark but two, and Paul employs it but twice in his ministry, while John and James in their epistles never allude to it? Such silence is an unanswerable refutation of all attempts to foist the meaning of endlessness into the word. "Everlasting fire" occurs three times, "everlasting destruction," once, "everlasting punishment" once, and "eternal damnation" once only. Shall any one suppose that the New Testament reveals endless torment, and that out of one hundred and ninety-nine occurrences of the word *aiōn*, it is applied to punishment so seldom, and that so many of those who wrote the New Testament never use the word at all? No. The New Testament usage agrees with the meaning in the Greek Classics, and in the Old Testament. Does it not strike the candid mind as impossible that God should have concealed this doctrine for thousands of years, and that for forty centuries of revelation he continually employed to teach limited duration the identical word that he at length stretched into the signification of endless duration? The word means limited duration all through the Old Testament; it never had the meaning of endless duration among those who spoke the Greek language (as we have demonstrated), but Jesus announced the doctrine of endless punishment, and selected as the word to convey his meaning the very word that in the Classics and Septuagint never contained any such thought, when there were several words in the copious Greek tongue that unequivocally conveyed the idea of interminable duration! Even if Matthew wrote in Hebrew or in Aramaic, he gave a Greek version of his gospel, and in that rejected every word that carries the meaning of endlessness, and appropriated the one which taught nothing of the kind. If this were the blunder of an incompetent translator, or the imperfect record of a reckless scribe, we could understand it, but to say that the inspired pen of the evangelist has deliberately or carelessly jeoparded the immortal welfare of countless millions by employing a word to teach the doctrine of ceaseless woe that up to that very hour taught only limited duration, is to make a declaration that carries its own refutation.

We come now to the sheet-anchor of the great heresy of the partialist church, the principal proof-text of an error hoary with antiquity, and not yet wholly abandoned—endless punishment. Matt. xxv: 46, "These shall go away into everlasting punishment, and the righteous into life eternal." We shall endeavor to establish several points against the erroneous view of this Scripture. 1. The whole account is a parable. 2. The punishment is not for unbelief, but for not benefiting the needy. 3. The general antecedent usage of the word denoting duration, proves that the duration is limited. 4. One object of punishment being to improve the punished, the punishment must be limited. 5. The events here described took place in this world, and must therefore be of limited duration. 6. The Greek word *kolasin*, rendered punishment, should be translated chastisement, as reformation is implied in its meaning.

1. The account is generally regarded as a literal description, but a careful reading shows that it is a parable,—"He will set the sheep on the right and the goats on the left." The sheep shall go into life eternal, and the goats into everlasting punishment. The sheep fed the hungry, clothed the naked, etc., while the goats were wanting in these kind offices. A kingdom was prepared for the sheep; but the goats were to be penned with the devil. The entire account is a parable.

2. The æonian punishment is for evil works. Practical benevolence is the virtue whose reward is here announced, and unkindness is the vice whose punishment is here threatened, and not faith and unbelief, on which heaven and hell are popularly predicated. Matt. xxv: 34-45, "Then shall the King say unto them on his right hand, Come, ye blessed of my Father, inherit the kingdom prepared for you from the foundation of the world: for I was a hungered, and ye gave me meat: I was thirsty, and ye gave me drink: I was a stranger, and ye took me in: naked, and ye clothed me: I was sick, and ye visited me: I was in prison, and ye came unto me. Then shall

the righteous answer him, saying, Lord, when saw we thee a hungered, and fed thee? or thirsty, and gave thee drink? When saw we thee a stranger, and took thee in? or naked, and clothed thee? Or when saw we thee sick, or in prison, and came unto thee? And the King shall answer and say unto them, Verily I say unto you, Inasmuch as ye have done it unto one of the least of these my brethren, ye have done it unto me. Then shall he say unto them on the left hand, Depart from me, ye cursed, into everlasting fire, prepared for the devil and his angels: for I was a hungered, and ye gave me no meat: I was thirsty, and ye gave me no drink: I was a stranger and ye took me not in: naked, and ye clothed me not: sick, and in prison, and ye visited me not. Then shall they also answer him, saying, Lord, when saw we thee a hungered, or athirst, or a stranger, or naked, or sick, or in prison, and did not minister unto thee? Then shall he answer them, saying, Verily I say unto you, Inasmuch as ye did it not to one of the least of these, ye did it not to me." If cruelty to the poor —neglect of them, even,—constitutes rejection of Christ—as is plainly taught here—and all who are guilty are to suffer endless torment, "who, then, can be saved?" The single consideration that works and not faith are here made the test of discipleship, cuts away the foundation of the popular view of this text.

3. The word *aiōnion* denotes limited duration. This has appeared in Classic and Old Testament Usage. It is impossible that Jesus should have used the word rendered everlasting in a different sense than we have shown to have been its meaning in antecedent literature.

4. God's punishments are remedial. All God's punishments are those of a Father, and must therefore be adapted to the improvement of his children. Heb. xii: 5, "My son, despise not thou the chastening of the Lord, nor faint when thou art rebuked of him: for whom the Lord loveth he chasteneth, and scourgeth every son whom he receiveth. If ye endure chastening, God dealeth with you as with sons: for what son is he whom the father chasteneth not? Furthermore, we have had fathers of our flesh which corrected us, and we

gave them reverence. Shall we not much rather be in subjection to the Father of spirits, and live? For they verily for a
few days chastened us after their own pleasure; but he for our
profit that we might be partakers of his holiness. Now, no
chastening for the present seemeth to be joyous, but grievous;
nevertheless, afterward it yieldeth the peaceable fruit of
righteousness unto them which are exercised thereby." Prov.
iii: 11, 12, "My son, despise not the chastening of the Lord;
neither be weary of his correction: for whom the Lord loveth
he correcteth; even as a father the son in whom he delight-
eth." Lam. iii: 31, 33, "For the Lord will not cast off forever:
but though he cause grief, yet will he have compassion according to the multitude of his mercies. For he doth not afflict
willingly, nor grieve the children of men." See also Job v;
Lev. xxvi; Psalms cxix: 67, 71, 75; Jer. ii: 19.

5. These events have occurred. The events here described
took place in this world within thirty years of the time when
Jesus spoke. They are now past. In Matt. xxiv: 4, the disciples asked our Lord when the then existing age would end.
The word (*aiōn*) is unfortunately translated world. Had he
meant world he would have employed *kosmos*, which means
world, as *aiōn* does not. After describing the particulars, he
announced that they would all be fulfilled, and the *aiōn* end
in that generation, before some of his auditors should die. If
he was correct the end came then. And this is demonstrated
by a careful study of the entire discourse, running through
Matt. xxiv and xxv. The disciples asked Jesus how they
should know his coming and the *end* of the age. They did not
inquire concerning the end of the actual world, as it is incorrectly translated, but age. This question Jesus answered by
describing the signs so that they, his questioners, the disciples
themselves, might perceive the approach of the end of the Jewish
dispensation (*aiōn*). He speaks fifteen times in the discourse
of his speedy coming (Matt. xxiv: 3, 27, 30, 37, 39, 42, 46, 48,
50, and xxv: 6, 10, 13, 19, 27, 31). He addresses those who
shall be alive at his coming (Matt. xxiv: 6, 20, 33, 34), "Ye shall
hear of wars, etc. Pray that your flight be not in the winter.

So likewise ye, when ye shall see all these things, know that it is near, even at the doors. Verily I say unto you, This generation shall not pass, till all these things be fulfilled." Campbell, Clarke, Wakefield, and Newton[6] translate the phrase, "end of the world" (*sunteleias tou aiōnos*) "conclusion of the age," "end of this dispensation." The question was, then, what shall indicate thy second coming and the end of the Mosaic economy (*aiōn*)? "When shall all these things be fulfilled?" Mark xiii: 1, 34. He spoke of the temple (Luke xxi: 5, 7), saying one stone should not be left on another, and the question of his disciples was, how shall we know when this is to take place? The answer is (Matt. xxiv: 6, 15, 20), "Ye shall hear of wars. Ye shall see the abomination of desolation. Pray that your flight be not in winter." The adverbs "then" and "when" connect all the events related in the two chapters in one unbroken series. And what infallible token did he give that these events would occur "then?" Matt. xxiv: 34, "Verily I say unto you, this generation shall not pass till all these things be fulfilled." What things? The "son of man coming in his glory in the clouds," and the end of the existing *aiōn*, or age. Mark phrases it, "This generation shall not pass till all these things be done." See Luke xxi: 25, 32. This whole account is a parable describing the end of the Jewish *aiōn*, age, or economy, signalized by the destruction of Jerusalem, and the establishment of the new *aiōn*, world, or age to come, that is, the Christian dispensation. Now on the authority of Jesus himself the *aiōn* then existing ended within a generation, namely, about A. D. 70. Hence, those who were sent away into *aiōnion* punishment, or the punishment of that *aiōn*, were sent into a condition corresponding in duration to the meaning of the word *aiōn*, i. e., age-lasting. A punishment cannot be endless, when defined by an adjective derived from a noun describing an event, the end of which is distinctly stated to have come.

6. The word translated punishment means improvement.

---

6 Com. in Loc.

The word is κόλασιν. It is thus authoritatively defined: [7]—
"Chastisement, punishment." "The trimming of the luxuriant
branches of a tree or vine to improve it and make it fruitful."
"The act of clipping or pruning—restriction, restraint, reproof,
check, chastisement."   "The kind of punishment which tends
to the improvement of the criminal, is what the Greek philosophers called *kolasis* or chastisement." "Pruning, checking,
punishment, chastisement, correction." "Do we want to know
what was uppermost in the minds of those who formed the
word for punishment? The Latin *pœna* or *punio*, to punish,
the root *pu* in Sanscrit, which means to cleanse, to purify,
tells us that the Latin derivation was originally formed, not
to express mere striking or torture, but cleansing, correcting,
delivering from the stain of sin." That it had this meaning in
Greek usage, we cite Plato: [8]—"For the natural or accidental
evils of others, no one gets angry, or admonishes, or teaches,
or punishes (*kolazei*) them, but we pity those afflicted with
such misfortune. . . For if, O Socrates, you will consider
what is the design of punishing (*kolazein*) the wicked, this
of itself will show you that men think virtue something that
may be acquired; for no one punishes (*kolazei*) the wicked
looking to the past only, simply for the wrong he has done,—
that is, no one does this thing who does not act like a wild
beast, desiring only revenge, without thought,—hence he who
seeks to punish (*kolazein*) with reason, does not punish for
the sake of the past wrong deed, . . but for the sake of the
future, that neither the man himself who is punished may do
wrong again, nor any other who has seen him chastised. And
he who entertains this thought, must believe that virtue may
be taught, and he punishes (*kolazei*) for the purpose of deter-
ring from wickedness." Like many other words this is not
always used in its exact and full sense: the Apocrypha
employs it as the synonym of suffering, regardless of reformation. See Wis. iii: 11, xvi: 1; I. Mac. vii: 7. See also Jose-

---

[7] Greenfield, Hedericus, Donnegan, Grotius, Liddell, Max Müller.

[8] Protag. Sec. 38, Vol I., p. 252.

phus.[9] It is found but four times in the New Testament. Acts iv: 21, the Jews let John and Peter go, "finding nothing further how they might punish them" (*kolasontai*). Did they not aim to reform them? Was not their punishment to cause them to return to the Jewish fold? From their standpoint the word was certainly used to convey the idea of reformation. I. John iv: 18, "Fear hath torment." Here the word "torment" should be restraint. It is thus translated in the Emphatic Diaglot. The idea is, if we have perfect love we do not fear God, but if we fear we are restrained from loving him. "Fear hath restraint." The word is used here with but one of its meanings. In II. Peter ii: 9, the apostle uses the word as our Lord did: the unjust are reserved unto the day of judgment to be punished (*kolazomenous*). This accords exactly with the lexicography of the word, and the general usage in the Bible and in Greek literature agrees with the meaning given by the lexicographers. Now, though the word rendered punishment is sometimes used to signify suffering alone, by Josephus and others, surely Divine inspiration will use it in its exact sense. We must therefore be certain that in the New Testament, when used by Jesus to designate divine punishment, it is generally used with its full meaning. The lexicographers and Plato, above, show us what that is, suffering, restraint, followed by correction, improvement. From this meaning of the word, torment is by no means excluded. God does indeed torment his children when they go astray. He is a "consuming fire," and burns with terrible severity towards us when we sin, but it is not because he hates, but because he loves us. He is a refiner's fire tormenting the immortal gold of humanity in the crucible of punishment, until the dross of sin is purged away. Mal. iii: 2, 3, "But who may abide the day of his coming? and who shall stand when he appeareth? for he is like a refiner's fire and like fuller's soap. And he shall sit as a refiner and purifier of silver: and he shall purify the sons of Levi, and purge them as gold or silver, that they may offer unto the

---

[9] War. III., V., VIII.; Ant. II., IV., V.

Lord an offering in righteousness." Therefore *kolasis* is just
the word to describe his punishments. They do for the soul
what pruning does for the tree, what the crucible of the refiner
does for the silver ore.

This should be further evident because of the nature of
punishment. Punishment is a means to an end. It is suffering administered as a penalty for the purpose of accomplish-
ing good results. The difference between revenge and punishment is this: Revenge is suffering inflicted with no good
end in view. Punishment is suffering inflicted for a good
purpose. Punishment aims at three objects: 1, the prevention
of the sin; 2, the reformation of the sinner; 3, the general
good Endless suffering can in no just sense of the word be
punishment, for it accomplishes no one of these results. It
does not prevent, but perpetuates sin; it does not reform, if
it is endless; it does not promote the general good,
for, if the general good is damaged by temporal sin,
it must be infinitely more injured by endless sinfulness.
Besides, all divine punishment must aim at the good of the
sinner, for it proceeds from him who only smites to bless. He
is a Father. Men are his children. Their sins exile them from
the true object of being. His punishments must, from the
nature of the case, and from the fact that he inflicts them, seek
to accomplish human good, and therefore must be finite in
duration, and end in reformation.[10]

The author of the "Emphatic Diaglot" gives this as the
literal rendering of the Greek,[11] "And these shall go forth to
the aionian cutting off, but the righteous to the aionian
life." And to this verse he appends this comprehensive and
suggestive note:—"The common version, and many modern ones, render *kolasin aiōnion*, everlasting punishment;

[10] "Since in all Greek literature, sacred and profane, *aiōnios* is applied to
things that end ten times as often as it is to things immortal, no fair critic
can assert positively that when it is connected with future punishment it
has the stringent meaning of metaphysical endlessness." Alger. Hist. Doct.
Fut. Life, p. 323.

[11] S. R. Wells, New York, 1873.

conveying the idea, as generally interpreted, of *basinos*, torment. *Kolasin*, in its various forms, occurs in three other places in the New Testament—Acts iv: 21; II. Peter ii: 9; I. John iv: 18. It is derived from *kolazoo*, which signifies, 1. To cut off, as lopping off branches of trees,—to prune. 2. To restrain, to repress. The Greeks write, 'The charioteer (*kolazoo*) restrains his fiery steed.' 3. To chastise, to punish. To cut off an individual from life, or society, or even to restrain, is esteemed as punishment; hence has arisen the third metaphorical use of the word. The primary signification has been adopted, because it agrees better with the second member of the sentence, thus preserving the force and beauty of the antithesis. 'The righteous go to life, the wicked to the cutting off from life, or death.'" See II. Thess. i: 9.

Even if *aiōnion* and *kolasis* were both of doubtful signification, and were we only uncertain as to their meaning, we ought to give God the benefit of the doubt, and understand the word in a way to honor him, that is, in a limited sense; but when all but universal usage ascribes to *aiōnion* limited duration, and the word *kolasin* is declared by all authorities to mean pruning, discipline, it is astonishing that Christian teachers should be found to imagine that when both words are together, they can mean anything else than temporary punishment ending in reformation, especially in a discourse in which it is expressly declared that the complete fulfillment was in this life, and within a generation of the time when the prediction was uttered.

Says Canon Farrar ("Excursus" in "Eternal Hope"):— "That in this instance the substantive *kolasis* is a word which in its sole proper meaning 'has reference to the correction and bettering of him that endures' (see Philo. Leg. ad Cai. I). So that Clement of Alexandria defines *kolaseis* as *merikai paideiai*. Archbishop Trench does indeed remark (New Testament Synonyms, p. 30) that 'It would be a very serious error to transfer this distinction of *kolasis* and *timoria* to the words as employed in the New Testament.' Why should it be a serious error to refrain from reading into a word a

8

sense which it does not possess? According to Aristotle *kolasis* is corrective, *timoria* alone is vindictive; *kolasis* has in view the improvement of the offender, *timoria* the satisfaction of the inflictor (ἡ μὲν κόλασις τοῦ πάσχοντος ἐνεκά ἐστιν· ἡ δε τιμωρία τοῦ ποιοῦντος ἵνα ἀποπληρωθῇ.—*Rhet. i: 10, 17*). It is Josephus, not our Lord and his apostles, who uses such phrases as *athanatos timoria* and *eirgmos aïdios*; and though 'everlasting death' occurs in our liturgy, it nowhere occurs in Scripture, frequently as we read of æonian life."

Says Rev. Prof. Plumtre, in a letter concerning Canon Farrar's sermons:—"There were two words which the Evangelist might have used,—*kolasis, timoria*. Of these the first carries with it, by the definition of the greatest of Greek ethical writers, the idea of a reformatory process. It is inflicted 'for the sake of him who suffers it.'[12] The second, on the other hand, describes a penalty purely vindictive or retributive. St. Matthew chose—if we believe that our Lord spoke Greek, he himself chose—the former word and not the latter."

Dean Trench says:[13]—"*Kolasin—timoria. Timoria* once (Heb. x: 29), *kolasin*, (Matt. xxv: 46; I. John iv: 18). *Timoria* is vindictive punishment, Latin, *ultio*, to satisfy the punished, from *timee* and *ouros*, protecting honor. *Kolasis*, to correct and better the punished, *castigatio*, Plato (Protag, 323 e). See also Clemens of Alexandria, Strom. iv: 24, Aristotle, Rhet. i: 10." Trench assumes that *kolasin* in Matt. xxv: 46, is not the same as usual, giving no reason but his own opinion that *kolasin aiōnion* in Matthew is exactly the same as *athanatos timoria* in Josephus, (B. J. ii: 8-11) and *aïdios timoria* of Plato (Ax. 372, a), which Jesus threatens (Mark ix: 43-48). See also the same idea in Josephus (Ant. xv: 22), Philo. (De Agricul. 9, Mart. Pol. 2), II. Macc. iv: 38; Wisd. Sol. xix: 4." This gratuitous opinion shows how easily the critic may be swamped in the theologian.

Rev. Samuel Cox, author of "Salvator Mundi," says in his "Doctrine of the Æons:"—"When our Lord speaks of the worm and the fire, we must take him to mean either the actual worm and the actual fire of the Gehenna valley, or some spiritual analogue of these, some discipline, some torment, which effects in the spiritual world, what the real worm and the real fire do in the natural world. The function of worms in the natural world is to prevent, though they seem to promote, putrefaction. They feed on the noxious matter which would else breed infection; they transmute the refuse of decay into their own living and healthy organisms. Fire, again, consumes dead and noxious matter, leaving only the ash, which is the best manure of a new crop, transmuting all else into higher and invisible forms. To rid the earth of that which is noxious and infectious, to transmute it into vital and wholesome forms—this is the proper function of both worm and fire in the natural world. What, then, can the moral analogue of them be, but a discipline so searching, so severe, as that it shall destroy that which is corrupt and corrupting, render innoxious that which is noxious, and evolve life itself from the very jaws of death? Here, then, our Lord explains his own thought to us, and shows us that the fire of Gehenna, the æonial fire, which he had in view, was the symbol, not of a vindictive and degrading punishment, but of a purifying and vivifying correction. 'Our God is a consuming fire,' and a fire that will burn until all that is evil is burned up."

It ought not to be forgotten that the oriental shepherd regards his goats as nearly as valuable as his sheep, and our Lord intimates this when he gives them the next best place to his right hand, namely, his left hand. And he speaks of them tenderly, for the word (ἐρίφων) is not "goats," but " kids," in verse 32, and in verse 33 even "kidlings" (ἐρίφια). The language is not that of anger, hatred, but of sympathy and kindness, as though Jesus had said the unfortunate goats shall be consigned to a severe but disciplinary punishment that shall purify and perfect them.

The stereotyped objection to these views originated with St. Augustine,[14] who said, "If we do not understand *aiōnios*

---

[14] A. D. 414.—De Civ. Dei XXI., 23. "*Dicere autem in hoc uno eodemque sensu, vita æterna sine fine erit, supplicium æternum finem habebit, multum absur-*

kolasis to mean endless punishment, we ought not to understand *aiōnios zoe* to mean everlasting life." This does not
follow, for the word is used in Greek in different senses in the
same sentence; as Hab. iii: 6, "And the *everlasting* mountains were scattered—his ways are *everlasting*." Suppose we
apply the popular argument here. The mountains and God
must be of equal duration, for the same word is applied to
both. Both are temporal or both are endless. But the mountains are expressly stated to be temporal—they "were scattered,"—therefore God is not eternal. Or God is eternal and
therefore the mountains must be. But they cannot be, for
they were scattered. The argument does not hold water. The
aiōnion mountains were destroyed. Hence the word may
denote both limited and unlimited duration in the same passage, the different meanings to be determined by the subject
treated. Canon Farrar observes: [15]—"The word 'æonian,'
though sanctioned by Mr. Tennyson in the lines—

> 'Draw down æonian hills, and sow
> The dust of continents to be,'

and though rendered very desirable by the sad confusion of
eternity with the mere negative conception of endlessness, can
perhaps hardly be naturalized. It is not worth while once
more to discuss its meaning when it has been so ably proved
by so many writers that there is no authority whatever for rendering it 'everlasting,' and when even those who, like Dr·
Pusey, are such earnest defenders of the doctrine of an endless hell, yet admit that the word only means 'endless within
the sphere of its own existence,' so that on their own showing
the word does not prove their point, and is, for instance, pow-
erless against those who hold the doctrine of conditional
immortality. It may be worth while, however, to point out once
more to less educated readers that *aiὼn aiώνιος* and their Hebrew
equivalents, in all combinations, are repeatedly used of things

---

dum est." Augustine also says that the whole human race is "one damned
batch and mass of perdition !" (*conspersio damnata, massa perditionis*.)

[15] Excursus on *Aiōnios*.

which have come and shall come to an end. Even Augustine admits (what, indeed, no one can deny) that in Scripture αἰὼν αἰώνιος must in many instances mean 'having an end'; and St. Gregory of Nyssa, who at least knew Greek, uses αἰώνιος as the epithet of 'an interval.' In answer to the old argument invented by St. Augustine (see note 14), and since his day so incessantly repeated,—the argument, namely, that if we do not make αἰώνιος κόλασις mean endless punishment we have no security that αἰώνιος ζωή means endless life, and that we thus lose our promise of everlasting happiness, I reply—1. This is absolutely no argument whatever, and ought never to be heard again, because the very men who most insist upon it, contemptuously set it aside, if we ask them to apply identically the same argument, analogously, to such texts as 'As in Adam all die, even so in Christ shall all be made alive.' 2. That our sure and certain hope of everlasting happiness rests on no such miserable foundation as the disputed meaning of a Greek adjective which is used over and over again of things transitory. If we need texts on which to rest it, we may find plenty, such as Luke xx: 36; Hos. xiii: 14; Rev. xxi: 4; Is. xxv: 6; I. Cor. xv, *passim*, etc. 3. That although we take the word *aiōnios* in both clauses to mean 'eternal'—by which (in this connection) we mean something above and beyond time, time being simply a mode of thought necessary only to our finite condition—(See John v: 39, xvii: 3)—yet it is by no means necessarily the case that the word should have identically the same meaning in both clauses, since the meaning of the same adjective might quite conceivably be modified, and even altered, by that of the substantive to which it is attached. Nothing could be more in accordance with the ordinary genius of human speech than that the same adjective might have its fullest meaning in one clause, in which that meaning is entirely consonant with reason and conscience, yet not have it in the other, where it would be shocking and terrible. What makes the argument as absolutely inexcusable on philological as it is on all other grounds, is, that in Rom. xvi: 25, 26, this very word occurs twice, and

in one of the two clauses cannot mean 'everlasting,' since it
is speaking of time which has come to an end; and it is yet
translated 'everlasting' by our translators in the very next
clause!—'According to the revelation of a mystery hidden in
silence in the eternal times' (E. V., 'before the *world* began,'
where the reader will see that 'endless' would be a fla-
grant absurdity), 'but now made manifest according to the
command of the *Eternal* God.'   But surely there are other
grounds on which we ought to have heard the last of this
dreary argument, to which it is hardly possible to listen without indignation. Good men, from St. Augustine to St. Thomas
Aquinas (Summ. part iii., Suppl., Quaest. 99, iii), and from
St. Thomas to Dr. Pusey, have gone on repeating it *ad nau-
seam*, and even the gentle Keble wrote—

> 'And if the treasures of thy wrath could waste,
> Thy lovers must their promised heaven forego.'

We hear the questions asked triumphantly in sermons, 'If the
punishment of the wicked is not to last forever, what guaran-
tee have we that the felicity of the blessed will last forever?'
I reply, Is there not in the question—when not traditionally
repeated, but plainly considered—an intense selfishness and a
most ignoble thought of God?"

Æonian punishment and life are coupled in the same passage only twice in the entire Bible, Dan. xii: 2, and Matt.
xxv: 46, and in Daniel the everlasting life and the everlasting
shame and contempt are expressly applied to temporal affairs,
namely, the destruction of Jerusalem.

The word may mean endless when applied to life, and not
when applied to punishment, even in the same sentence,
though we think duration is not considered so much as the
intensity of the joy or the sorrow, in either case.   The epithet
in such instances is qualitative rather than quantitative.

Therefore, 1, the fulfillment of the language in this life;
2, the meaning of *aiōnion*; and, 3, the meaning of *kolasis*,
demonstrate that the penalty threatened in Matt. xxv: 46 is
a limited one.   It is a threefold cord that human skill cannot

break.   Prof. Tayler Lewis thus translates Matt. xxv: 46,
"These shall go away into the punishment (the restraint, imprisonment) of the world to come, and those into the life of the
world to come."   And he says *"that is all that we can etymologically or exegetically make of the word in this passage."*
Hence, also, the *zoen aiōnion* (life eternal) is not endless,
but is a condition resulting from a good character.   The intent
of the phrase is not to teach immortal happiness, nor does
kolasin aiōnion indicate endless punishment.   Both phrases,
regardless of duration, refer to the limited results of wrong-
ing or blessing others, extending possibly through Messiah's
reign until "the end" (I. Cor. xv.).   Both describe consequences of conduct to befall those referred to at his "coming,"
then "at hand," and all those consequences antedate the
immortal state.

Canon Kingsley, author of "Hypatia,"etc., observes ("Mem-
oirs"), "The word (*aiōn, æon*) is never used in Scripture or anywhere else in the sense of endlessness (vulgarly called eternity).   It always meant, both in Scripture and out, a period
of time.   Else, how could it have a plural—how could you talk
of the *æons*, and *æons* of *æons*, as the Scripture does?
Aiōnios therefore means, and must mean, belonging to an
epoch, or the epoch; and *aiōnios kolasis* is the punishment
allotted to that epoch."

But the blessed life has not been left dependent on so
equivocal a word.   The soul's immortal and happy existence
is taught in the New Testament by words that in the Bible
are never attached to anything that is of limited duration.
They are applied to God and the soul's happy existence only.
These words are *akataluton*, imperishable; *amarantos* and
amarantinos, unfading; *aphtharto*, immortal, incorruptible;
and *athanasian*, immortality.   Let us quote some of the passages in which these words occur.—Heb. vii: 16, "And it is yet
far more evident: for that after the similitude of Melchizedec
there ariseth another priest, who is made, not after the law of
a carnal commandment, but after the power of an *endless*
(*akatalutos*, imperishable) life."   I. Pet. i: 3, 4, "Blessed be

the God and Father of our Lord Jesus Christ, which according to his abundant mercy, hath begotten us again unto a lively hope by the resurrection of Jesus Christ from the dead, to an inheritance *incorruptible (aphtharton)* and undefiled, and that *fadeth not (amaranton)* away." I. Pet. v: 4, "And when the chief shepherd shall appear, ye shall receive a crown of glory that *fadeth not (amarantinos)* away." I. Tim. i: 17, "Now unto the King eternal, *immortal (aphtharto)*, invisible, the only wise God, be honor and glory forever and ever, Amen." Rom. i: 23, "And changed the glory of the *incorruptible* God into an image made like to corruptible man." I. Cor. ix: 25, "Now they do it to obtain a corruptible crown; but we an *incorruptible.*" I. Cor. xv: 51, 54, "Behold, I shew you a mystery; we shall not all sleep, but we shall all be changed in a moment, in the twinkling of an eye, at the last trump: for the trumpet shall sound, and the dead shall be raised *incorruptible (aphthartoi)*, and we shall be changed. For this corruptible must put on *incorruption (aphtharsian)*, and this mortal must put on *immortality (athanasian)*. So when this corruptible shall have put on *incorruption (athanasian)*, and this mortal shall have put on *immortality (aphtharsian)*, then shall be brought to pass the saying that is written, Death is swallowed up in victory." Rom. ii: 7, "To them who by patient continuance in well doing seek for glory and honor and *immortality (aphtharsia)*, eternal life." I. Cor. xv: 42, "So also is the resurrection of the dead. It is sown in corruption, it is raised in *incorruption (aphtharsia).*" See also verse 50. II. Tim. i: 10, "Who brought life and *immortality (aphtharsian)* to light, through the gospel." I. Tim. vi: 16, "Who only hath *immortality (athanasian).*"

The terms *athanatos, adialeiptos* and *aïdios* definitely and unequivocally denote endlessness. These words were in common use by the contemporaries of Jesus. *These words Jesus never used.* That is to say, he avoided the only phraseology that unequivocally teaches endlessness, when applied to punishment, and the very terms then in common use.

A very much stronger word is *aperantos,* endless, interminable, found in I. Tim. i: 4, "endless genealogies," though it is sometimes used hyperbolically, as here. Another stronger word is *akatalutos*,[16] indissoluble, as in Heb. vii: 16, "endless life." Had it been intended to express the interminable duration of punishment, would not these strong words have been employed, instead of so equivocal a one as the subject of this biography? And does not the fact that the New Testament authors absolutely refused to employ those stronger words when describing the duration of punishment, demonstrate that they did not intend to teach its eternity?

Now, these words the Greeks rarely used, except to denote endlessness. Perhaps the strongest of Greek words is *ateleutetos*.[17] It is never found in the New Testament, though it was used by the Emperor Justinian, in his letter to the patriarch Mennas, when he desired to declare the endlessness of punishment by a word entirely unambiguous. He says,[18] "The holy church of Christ teaches an endless æonian life for the righteous, and an endless punishment for the wicked." He does not rest the eternity of life on the word *aiōnios*, but adds *ateleutetos* to it, and when announcing the eternity of future punishment, he does not depend on the word *aiōnios* at all, but considers *ateleutetos* sufficient of itself. Can any one doubt that this strongest of all words would have been used, had eternal punishment been in our Lord's mind? And how can any advocate of endless punishment account for the feebler word used, and the neglect of the stronger, except that he intended to teach no such doctrine?

The Greek language possesses, and the New Testament uses, words of vastly stronger import than the æonian phraseology, that are applied to what has no end, and these words might have been, shall we not say would have been,

[16] ἀκατάλυτος.

[17] ἀτελεύτητος.

[18] E. Beecher, D. D., Christian Union, Sept. 17, 1873.

connected with punishment had it been intended to teach its interminable duration? *Apeiros* signifies endless, unlimited, infinite. Aristotle employs it in the sense of endless. *Aperantos* is endless, infinite. *Aïdios*, eternal, perpetual, continual, everlasting. Paul thus employs it, God's "eternal power and Godhead." Jude speaks of *aïdios* chains, for exposition of which see Appendix B, of this volume.

Let us consider somewhat more minutely the several Greek words that are far stronger in their meaning than are the æonian terms, and that are rarely, and some of them never, in the Bible, applied to anything of temporary duration, and never to the punishment of human sinners.

1. Ἀΐδιος (*aïdios*) (*eternal, perpetual, everlasting*).[19] Paul applies it to God (Rom. i: 20), "his eternal power and Godhead" (ἥτε ἀΐδιος αὐτοῦ δύναμις καὶ θειότης). Jude (6) speaks of certain chains as eternal (δεσμοῖς ἀϊδίοις). [See Appendix B.] Aristotle observes,[20] "There are certain difficult questions which we cannot certainly determine, as whether or not the world is eternal (οἶον πότερον 'ο κόσμος ἀΐδιος ἢ οὔ). Here the word denotes absolute eternity.

2. Ἀμάραντος and Ἀμαράντινος (*amarantos, amarantinos*) (*unfading, fadeless, eternal*).[19] I. Pet. i: 4, "An inheritance incorruptible and undefiled, and that fadeth not away" (εἰς κληρονομίαν ἄφθαρτον καὶ ἀμίαντον καὶ ἀμάραντον).

3. Ἀθάνατος (*athanatos*) (*immortal, deathless, never-dying*).[19] The noun of this adjective, *athanasia*, occurs in I. Cor. xv: 54, "This mortal must put on immortality." Pythagoras applies it to the gods in his "Golden Sayings."[21]

4. Ἀκατάλυτος (*akatalutos*) (*indissoluble, incapable of being destroyed*).[19] Heb. vii: 16, "an endless life" (ζωῆς ἀκαταλύτου).

5. Ἄφθαρτος (*aphthartos*) (*incorruptible, immortal, eternal*).[19] In I. Tim. i: 17, God is *aphthartō*. In I. Pet. i: 4,

---

19 Ewing, Grove.
20 Trop. i: 11.
21 Græca Majora, pp. 241, 312-314.

the soul's life is *aphtharton*. In Rom. i: 23, God is incorruptible, *aphthartou*. In I. Cor. ix: 25, the reward of Christian effort is imperishable, *aphtharton*. In I. Cor. xv: 52, the dead are to experience an incorruptible life, *aphthartoi*. In I. Pet. i: 23, the happy life hereafter is *aphthartou*.

6. 'Ατερμων (*atermōn*) (*infinite, interminable*). Aristotle employs it to strengthen *aiōn*,[22] "From an interminable age to another age" (*ἐξ αἰῶνος ἀτέρμονος εἰς ἕτερον αἰῶνα*). This word is not in the Bible.

7. 'Απεραντος (*aperantos*) (*endless, boundless*).[23] I. Tim. i: 4, "endless genealogies" (*γενεαλογίαις ἀπεράντοις*). Justin Martyr defines the punishment of the wicked by the word,[24] *τὸν ἀπέραντον αἰῶνα*.

Let us quote the passages in which some of these words occur:—Heb. vii: 15, 16, "And it is yet far more evident: for that after the similitude of Melchizedec there ariseth another priest, who is made, not after the law of a carnal commandment, but after the power of an *endless* (*akatalutou*), (imperishable) life." I. Pet. i: 3, 4, "Blessed be the God and Father of our Lord Jesus Christ, which, according to his abundant mercy, hath begotten us again unto a lively hope by the resurrection of Jesus Christ from the dead, to an inheritance *incorruptible* (*aphtharton*), and undefiled, and that *fadeth not* (*amaranton*) away." I. Pet. v: 4, "And when the chief shepherd shall appear, ye shall receive a crown of glory that *fadeth not* (*amarantinon*) away." I. Tim. i: 17, "Now unto the King eternal, *immortal* (*aphtharto*), invisible, the only wise God, be honor and glory forever and ever, Amen." Rom. i: 23, "And changed the glory of the *incorruptible* (*aphthartou*) God into an image made like to corruptible man." I. Cor. ix: 25, "Now they do it to obtain a corruptible crown; but we an *incorruptible*" (*aphtharton*). I. Cor. xv: 51, 54, "Behold, I shew you a mystery; we shall not all sleep, but we shall be changed, in a moment, in the twinkling

---

[22] De Mundo.   [23] Ewing and Grove.   [24] Apol. I., C, 27.

of an eye, at the last trump: for the trumpet shall sound, and the dead shall be raised *incorruptible* (*aphthartoi*), and we shall be changed. For this corruptible must put on *incorruption* (*aphtharsian*), and this mortal must put on *immortality* (*athanasian*). So, when this corruptible shall have put on *incorruption* (*aphtharsian*), and this mortal shall have put on *immortality* (*athanasian*), then shall be brought to pass the saying that is written, death is swallowed up in victory." Rom. ii: 7, "To them who by patient continuance in well doing seek for glory and honor and *immortality* (*athanasian*), eternal life." I. Cor. xv: 42, "So also is the resurrection of the dead. It is sown in corruption, it is raised in *incorruption* (*aphtharsia*)." See also verse 50. II. Tim. i: 10, "Who brought life and *immortality* (*aphtharsian*) to light, through the gospel." I. Tim. vi: 16, "Who only hath *immortality* (*athanasian*)."

The way in which men may honestly and unconsciously carry an error, even when they really know better, is happily illustrated in the following anecdote, which our friend, Rev. G. L. Demarest, has communicated:—"Many years ago, being clerk in a New York publishing house, I called to collect a note or a check for a running account, upon a bookseller who was a member of a Congregational church. I had hardly entered the store, before he asked me, 'Mr. D., how do you Universalists get over Matt. xxv: 46?' 'We don't "get over" it; we don't want to get over it; it suits us just as it is.' 'Why, doesn't that teach endless punishment?' 'Not at all: I suppose you depend on the word "everlasting," do you not?' 'Of course.' 'Well, the word there translated "everlasting" does not necessarily mean endless.' Just at the moment Professor Bush came in—Rev. George Bush, then in good standing in the Presbyterian church, author of notes on Genesis and other Old Testament books, Professor of Hebrew and Oriental Literature in the University of the State of New York, whom I knew personally as a most amiable Christian man, and honest and true. At once said my friend, 'Professor, Mr. D. says that the word translated "everlasting" in Matt. xxv: 46, does not necessarily mean "endless"; is that so?' 'Yes,' said Prof. B., 'that is so; but if the Savior intended to express the idea of endlessness, he could not have found a stronger word in Greek.' 'Professor,' said I, 'you surprise me; I thought *althanatos* stronger.' 'So it is.' 'I thought *akatalutos* stronger.' 'So it is.' 'I thought *aphthartos* stronger.' 'So IT IS.' I attended to the business upon which I called, and left." Here was a ripe scholar honestly insisting on what he knew to be false. Such is the power of habit, and the force of a false theological bias.

Now, these words are applied to God and the soul's happiness. They are never in the Bible applied to punishment, or to anything perishable. They would have been affixed to punishment had the Bible intended to teach endless punish-ment. And certainly they show the error of those who declare that the equivocal word *aiōnion* is all the word, or the strong-est word in the Bible, declarative of endless duration, or of the endlessness of the life beyond the grave. A little more study of the subject would prevent such reckless statements as are frequently made by men professing scholarship, and would show that the happy, endless life does not depend at all on the pet word of partialist critics.

Canon Farrar observes: [25]—"Thank God, my own hopes of seeing God's face for ever hereafter do not rest on ten times refuted attempts to read false meanings into the Greek lexicon in order to support a system far darker than St. Augustine's, from whose mistaken literalism it took its disastrous origin. But here I declare, and call God to witness, that if the popular doctrine of hell were true, I should be ready to resign all hope, not only of a shortened, but of any immortality, if thereby I could save, not millions, but one single human soul from what fear, and super-stition, and ignorance, and inveterate hate, and slavish letter-worship, have dreamed and thought of hell. I call God to witness that so far from regretting the possible loss of some

---

[25] Eternal Hope.

billions of *œons* of bliss by attaching to the word *aiōnios* a sense in which scores of times it is undeniably found, I would here, and now, and kneeling on my knees, ask him that I might die as the beasts that perish, and for ever cease to be, rather than that my worst enemy should endure the hell described by Tertullian, or Minucius Felix, or Jonathan Edwards, or Dr. Pusey, or Mr. Furniss, or Mr. Moody, or Mr. Spurgeon, for one single year. Unless my whole nature were utterly changed, I can imagine no immortality which would not be abhorrent to me if it was accompanied with the knowledge that the millions and millions and millions of poor suffering wretches—some of whom on earth I had known and loved—were writhing in an agony without end or hope."

The origin of the argument that endless punishment is taught in Matt. xxv : 46, because the same word describing the duration of life is used to describe the duration of punishment, is interesting.[26] Orosius, a Spanish Presbyter, visited Augustine, A. D. 413, and informed him that the Origenists affirmed that *aiōnios* denoted an indefinitely long, and not an endless, duration. Augustine replied in a letter that though *aiōn* could signify limited, *aiōnios* could not, as the Greeks only applied it to things without end. And referring to the æonian things in the Mosaic dispensation, he declared that they were eternal because the things they typify are eternal, and that in Matt. xxv : 46, endless duration is taught, both of life and punishment.[27] And yet he confesses, "I am not so accustomed to the Greek language that I am at all competent to read and understand books on such subjects." [28] "I have learned very little of the Greek language, and almost nothing." [29] And yet orthodox theologians for fourteen hundred years have bowed to the dictum of Augustine, though he confesses he was wholly incompetent to pronounce on the subject, and whose statement is contradicted by uniform Greek usage!

---

[26] Beecher, Hist. Fut. Ret., pp. 249-50.

[27] See also his "City of God," B. xxi. 23, and Manual of Theology, C. 112.

[28] De Trinitate iii, Proem.

[29] Contra literos Petiliani I., ii. C. 38.

If endless happiness were promised in the second member of this sentence, it would not follow that endless punishment is threatened in the first, for, as Dr. J. M. Whiton correctly observes,[30] "If it be antecedently as probable that God will evermore uphold in being a soul irrecoverably involved in the processess of 'æonian destruction' (II. Thess. i: 9), as it is that he will perpetuate, according to a specific promise (John xiv: 19), the immortality of a soul healthfully developing the 'æonian life' received through Christ; then, and not otherwise, the inference of an endless misery from an endless happiness, may have some rational foundation."

Clemance, an English writer,[31] declares that these Greek terms are "words which shine only by a reflected light. If good ever should come to an end, that would come to an end which Christ died to bring in, but if evil comes to an end, that comes to an end which he died to destroy. So that the two stand by no means on the same footing. An æon may have an end. Æons of æons may have an end. Only that which lasts through all the æons is without an end; and Scripture affirms this only of the Kingdom of God, and of the glory of God in the church. The absolute eternity of evil is nowhere affirmed."

The meaning of the terms "life eternal" and "life everlasting" (*zoen aiōnion*), can be ascertained by a little investigation.

1. *Zoen aiōnion* in the New Testament, is the life resulting from Christian faith. John iii: 36, "He that believeth on the son *hath* everlasting life;" 16, "Whosoever believeth in him should *have* everlasting life;" vi: 47, 54, "Verily, verily, I say unto you, he that believeth on me *hath* everlasting life. Whoso eateth my flesh, and drinketh my blood, *hath* eternal life;" John xvii: 3, "This is life eternal, to know thee, the only true God, and Jesus Christ, whom thou *hast* sent." See also, John x: 28, xiv: 50. This life may be, and often is, only

---

[30] Preface to Is Eternal Punishment Endless?
[31] Future Punishment, pp. 65-6, quoted by Canon Farrar

a temporary possession; men have it, and fall from grace and lose it. It denotes, therefore, the present enjoyment, or blessedness, of following Christ. John vi: 33, 53, "For the bread of God is he which cometh down from heaven, and giveth life unto the world. Then Jesus said unto them, verily, verily, I say unto you, except ye eat the flesh of the son of man, and drink his blood, ye have no life in you." See also I. John iii: 15, v: 12; John iii: 15, etc. The blessed life of the soul in the immortal world does not depend on faith here.

2. *Zoen aiŏnion* especially denotes the reward that was received by those who were faithful at the time of Christ. Matt. xix: 29, "And every one that hath forsaken houses, or brethren, or sisters, or father, or mother, or wife, or children, or lands, for my name's sake, shall receive a hundredfold, and shall inherit everlasting life." Mark x: 30, "But he shall receive a hundredfold now in this time, houses, and brethren, and sisters, and mothers, and children, and lands, with persecutions; and in the world to come, eternal life." Consult, also, Luke xviii: 30; John xii: 25; Matt. xxv: 46. As this eternal life was to be given as a reward, it cannot mean the immortal life, for that life is a "free gift."

3. *Zoen aiŏnion* sometimes denotes the immortal life of the soul hereafter. John xvii: 1, 2, "Father, the hour is come, glorify thy son, that thy son may also glorify thee, as thou hast given him power over all flesh that he might give eternal life to as many as thou hast given him." Rom. v: 21, "As sin hath reigned unto death, even so might grace reign through righteousness unto eternal life by Jesus Christ our Lord." I. John v: 11, "This is the record that God hath given us eternal life, and this life is in his son."

The life eternal, or everlasting, that is bestowed for faith, or obedience, is a present blessing. The future life is the "gift of God." But though sometimes used thus, it should always be borne in mind that this phrase "everlasting life" or "eternal life" does not usually denote endless existence, but the life of the gospel, spiritual life, the Christian life, regardless of its duration. In more than fifty of the seventy-two times that the adjective occurs in the New Testament, it describes life. John v: 24, "He that believeth on him that sent me *hath* everlasting life, and shall not come into condemnation, but is *passed* from death unto life." Eternal life is the life of the gospel. Its duration depends on the possessor's fidelity. It is no less the *aiōnion* life, if one abandon it in a month after acquiring it. It consists in knowing, loving and serving God. It is the Christian life, regardless of its duration. How often the good fall from grace. Believing, they have the *aiōnion* life, but they lose it by apostasy. Notoriously it is not, in thousands of cases, endless. The life is of an indefinite length, so that the usage of the phrase in the New Testament is altogether in favor of giving the word the sense of limited duration. Hence Jesus does not say, "he that believeth shall enjoy endless happiness," but "he hath everlasting life," and "is passed from death unto life."

It scarcely need here be proved that the *aiōnian* life can be acquired and lost. Heb. vi: 4, "For it is impossible for those who were once enlightened, and have tasted of the heavenly gift, and were made partakers of the holy ghost, and have tasted the good word of God, and the powers of the world to come, if they shall fall away, to renew them again unto repentance: seeing they crucify to themselves the son of God afresh, and put him to an open shame." A life that can thus be lost is not intrinsically endless. "Eternal life" with the sacred writers has less the sense of perpetuity, than of moral quality. It denotes spiritual regeneration. It is sometimes called "life" merely. Thus, "I come that ye may have life," "bread of life," "enter into life," "God hath given us eternal life and this life is in his son;" "He that hath the son, hath life." In all these the meaning indicates a life from moral death, a regeneration, having no reference to its duration.

It is often remarked that as, according to Josephus, the Jews in our Savior's time believed in endless punishment, Jesus must have taught the same doctrine, as "he employed the terms the Jews used." But this is not true, as we have

9

shown.   Christ and his apostles did not employ the phraseology that the Jews used to describe this doctrine.   As we have shown, Philo used *athanaton* and *ateleuteton*, meaning immortal, and interminable.   He says, [32] "to live always dying, and to undergo an immortal and interminable death."   He also employs *aïdion*, but not *aiōnion*. [33]   Josephus says, "They, the Pharisees, believe ' the souls of the bad are allotted *to an eternal prison*, and punished with *eternal retribution*."   In describing the doctrine of the Essenes, Josephus says they believe "the souls of the bad are sent to a dark and tempestuous cavern, full of *incessant punishment*."   But the phraseology of Jesus and the apostles is *kolasin aiōnion*, or *aiōnion kriseon*, "æonian chastisement," or "æonian condemnation."   The Jews contemporary with Jesus call retribution *aïdios*, or *adialeiptos timoria*, while the Savior calls it *aiōnios krisis* or *kolasis aiōnios*, and the apostles, *olethros aiōnios, æonian destruction*; and *puros aiōnios, æonian fire*.   Had Jesus and his apostles used the terms employed by the Jews to whom they spoke, we should be compelled to admit that they taught the popular doctrine.   See this point further elucidated, at the end of this volume, in appendix B., on the word *aïdios*.

"To live always dying and undergo an endless death," is the language of "orthodox" pulpits, and of the Greek Jews, but our Savior and his apostles carefully avoided charging God with being the author of so cruel a calamity.

Says a learned scholar: [34]—"*Aiōnios* is a word of sparing occurrence among ancient classical Greek writers; nor is it by any means the common term employed by them to signify *eternal*.   On the contrary, they much more frequently make use of *aïdios, aei on*, or some similar mode of speech, for this purpose.   .   .   .   To me it appears that the Seventy, by choosing *aiōnios* to represent *olam*, testify that they did not understand the Hebrew word to signify *eternal*.   Had

---

[32] Universalist Expositor, Vol. III., p. 446.
[33] Universalist Expositor, Vol. III., p. 437.
[34] Christian Examiner, Sept., 1830.

they so understood it, they would certainly have translated it by some more decisive word; some term, which, like *aïdios*, is more commonly employed in Greek, to signify that which has neither beginning nor end."

Moreover, the evidence is overwhelming that the auditors of Jesus, besides the Pharisees and Essenes, did not believe in endless punishment. Philipson declares,[35] "The Rabbins do not accept the eternity of hell torments."[36] The ancient Jewish authorities agree that endless punishment was not a doctrine of the Jews at the time of Christ, except as it was in some cases held by those who had obtained it of the heathen. To such Jesus referred when he denounced the "traditions" of the Pharisees. "There is a space of only two fingers' breadth between hell and heaven; the sinner has but to repent sincerely, and the gates to everlasting bliss will spring open."[37] "Gehenna is nothing but a day in which the impious shall be burned."[38] "The judgment of the ungodly is for twelve months."[39]

---

[35] Israelitische Religionslehre, ii : 255.

[36] "Die Rabbiner nehmen keine Ewigkeit der Höllenstrafen an, auch die grössten Sünder werden nur 'Generationen hindurch' gestraft." Quoted by Canon Farrar, who gives this valuable note from Stephelin's Rabbinical Literature (1748), II, 31, 71:—Zijoni, f. 69, 3, "only a thread's thickness between Paradise and Gehenna;" Asarath Maamaroth, f. 85, 1, "there will be no more Gehenna;" Jalkuth Shimoni, f. 46, 1, "Gabriel and Michael will open the 8,000 gates of Gehenna, and let out Israelites and righteous Gentiles;" Jalkuth Chadash, f. 57, 1, "The righteous bring out of heaven imperfect souls;" Jalkuth Rubeni, f. 167, 4, "Sabbaths and refrigeria of the doomed;" Zohar, in Exod. Tr. Gibborim, f. 70, 1; Nishmath Chajim, f. 83, 1; Jalkuth Shimoni, f. 83, 3, and many other passages speak of 12 months as the period of punishment in Gehenna. In a magnificent passage of Othoth (attributed to Akiba) it is said that God has a key of Gehenna, and that he will preach to all the righteous, that Zerubbabel will say the Kaddish and an Amen! shall sound forth from Gehenna, and that Gabriel and Michael will open the 40,000 gates of Gehenna, and set free the damned. Akiba founds this on Isa. xxvi: 2, reading Shomer Amenim "observing the Amen," for *Shomer Emunim*, "keeping the truth." Lastly, in *Emek Hammelech*, f. 138, 4, "the wicked stay in Gehenna till the resurrection, and then the Messiah, passing through it, redeems them." [See Appendix C.]

[37] Deutsch, Remains, p. 33.   [38] Abhoda, Zara. Rabbi Akiba.

[39] Adyoth, ii: 10, "Die Strafen in Gehenna. In diesem Punkt erklären

All these facts demonstrate that the Jews did not regard
the word *aiōnios* in the Scriptures as denoting endless duration, for they applied it to punishment, and yet they regarded
Gehenna, the place of future punishment, as of limited duration.

We will now consider the other passages in the New Testament, in which punishment, or the consequences of sin, are
declared to be æonian.

Matt. xii : 32, "Whosoever speaketh against the holy ghost,
it shall not be forgiven him, neither in this *world* (τουτω τω αἰῶνι,
this the age), neither in the world to come."   Parallel passages :
Mark iii : 29, "But he that shall blaspheme against the holy
ghost hath never forgiveness, but is in danger of eternal damnation."   Luke xii : 10, "And whosoever shall speak a word
against the son of man, it shall be forgiven him; but unto him
that blasphemeth against the holy ghost it shall not be forgiven."   Literally, "neither in this age nor the coming," that
is, neither in the Mosaic, nor the Christian age or dispensation.   But, then, these ages will both end, and in the dispensation of the fullness of times, or ages, all are to be redeemed.
(Eph. i : 10.)   The exact rendering of Mark iii : 29 is not,
"hath never forgiveness," but "hath not forgiveness for the
æon, but is involved in æonian sin." [40]   The parallel passage,
Matt. xii : 32, reads, "It shall not be forgiven him, neither in
this nor in the coming *æon*."   Luke xii : 10, "Shall not be forgiven."   The original of Mark iii : 29 so plainly teaches that
the penalty here threatened is of limited duration, that Augustine taught that those unforgiven in the present, would obtain
forgiveness in some future *aeon*.   He says (See Lange, Com.

---

sich die Talmudlehrer entschieden gegen die Annahme der Ewigkeit der
Höllenstrafen."   Hamburger Talmudisches Wörterbuch : S. V. Hölle.

[40] The Vat. MS. reads "transgression," and Griesbach has placed *amar-
temator* in the margin.   Grotius, Mille and Bengel prefer this reading, which
is according to the Coptic, Armenian, Gothic, Vulgate, and all the Itala, but
two.

Matt., pp. 227-229), "For it would not be truly said of some, that they are forgiven neither in this age (*seculo*) nor in the future, were there not some who, though not in this, are for-given in the future." If the future is to consist of *œons*, and *œons of œons*, and the sinner does not find forgiveness in this or the next, it by no means follows that he will not in some future *œon*. The thought of the Savior is, that those who should attribute his good deeds to an evil spirit would be so hardened that his religion would have greater difficulty in affect-ing them than when guilty of any other sin. Endless damnation is not thought of, and cannot be extorted from the lan-guage.

In the New Testament the "end of the age" and "ages" is a common expression, referring to what has now passed. See Col. i: 26; Heb. ix: 26; Matt. xiii: 39, 40, 49, xxiv: 3. Says Locke,[41] "The nation of the Jews were the kingdom and peo-ple of God whilst the law stood. And this kingdom of God, under the Mosaic constitution, was called *aiōn outos*, this age, or, as it is commonly translated, this world. But the kingdom of God, which was to be under the Messiah, wherein the economy and constitution of the Jewish church, and the nation itself, that in opposition to Christ adhered to it, was to be laid aside, is in the New Testament called *aiōn mellon*, the world or age to come." Another writer[42] adds, "Why the times under the law were called *kronoi aiōnioi*, we may find reason in their jubilees, which were *aiōnes*, 'secula,' or 'ages,' by which all the time under the law, was measured; and so *kronoi aiōnioi* is used, II. Tim. i: 9; Tit. i: 2. And so *aiōnes* are put for the times of the law, or the jubilees, Luke i: 70; Acts iii: 21; I. Cor. ii: 7, x: 11; Eph. iii: 9; Col. i: 26; Heb. ix: 26. And so God is called the rock of *aiōnos*, of age (Isa. xxvi: 4), in the same sense that he is called the rock of Israel (Isa. xxx: 29), *i. e.*, the strength and support of the Jewish state;—for it is of the Jews

[41] Notes on Galatians i.

[42] Burthog's Christianity a Revealed Mystery, pp. 17-18. Note on Rom. xvi: 23.

the prophet here speaks. So, Ex. xxi:6, *eis ton aiɔna* signifies, not as we translate it, 'forever,' but 'to the jubilee';
which will appear, if we compare Lev. xxv:39-41, and Ex.
xxi:2." Pearce,[43] in his commentary, says, "Rather, neither in
this age nor in the age to come, *i. e.*, neither in this age,
when the law of Moses subsists, nor in that, also, when the
kingdom of heaven, which is at hand, shall succeed to it. The
Greek *aiɔn* seems to signify age here, as it often does in the
New Testament (see chap. xiii:40, xxiv:3; Col. i:26; Eph.
iii:9, 21), and according to its most proper signification. If
this be so, then this age means the Jewish one, the age while
their law subsisted and was in force; and the age to come (see
Heb. vi:6; Eph. ii:9) means that under the Christian dispensation." Wakefield observes,[44] "Age, *aiɔni*; *i. e.*, the Jewish
dispensation, which was then in being, or the Christian, which
was going to be." Clarke,[45] "Though I follow the common
translation (Matt. xii:31, 32), yet I am fully satisfied the
meaning of the words is, neither in this dispensation, viz., the
Jewish, nor in that which is to come, the Christian. *Olam
ha-bo*, the world to come, is a constant phrase for the times of
the Messiah, in the Jewish writers." See also Hammond,
Rosenmüller, etc.[46] Take Hebrews ix:26, as an example:
"For then must he (Christ) often have suffered since the
foundation of the world (*kosmos*, literally world), but now once
in the end of the world (*aiɔnɔn*, ages) hath he appeared to
put away sin by the sacrifice of himself." What world was at
its end when Christ appeared? Indubitably the Jewish age.
The world or age to come (*aiɔn*) must be the Christian dispensation, as in I. Cor. x:11, where Paul says that upon him
and his contemporaries "the ends of the world are come."
These passages state in strong language the heinous nature
of the sin referred to. The age or world to come is not beyond
the grave, but it is the Christian dispensation. It had a

---

[43] Notes on Matt. xii:31-32.   [44] Com. in loco.

[45] Ibid.   [46] Paige's Selections.

beginning eighteen centuries ago, and it will end when Jesus shall have delivered the kingdom to God, the Father, and (I. Cor. xv) when God shall be all in all.

Matt. xviii: 8, "Wherefore, if thy hand or thy foot offend thee, cut them off, and cast them from thee: it is better for thee to enter into life halt or maimed, rather than having two hands, or two feet, to be cast into everlasting fire." Matt. xxv: 41 uses the same phraseology, "The everlasting fire, prepared for the devil and his angels." Also Jude 7, "Even as Sodom and Gomorrah, and the cities about them in like manner, giving themselves over to fornication, and going after strange flesh, are set forth for an example, suffering the vengeance of eternal fire." It is better to enter into the Christian life maimed, that is, be deprived of some apparent advantage comparable to an eye, foot, or hand, than to keep all worldly advantages, and suffer the penalty of rejecting Christ, typified by fire, is the meaning of Matt. xviii: 8; and Jude 7 teaches that Sodom and Gomorrah are an example of æonian fire. But that fire has expired. That the fire referred to is not endless, is shown by the use of the term in the Bible. "God is a consuming fire" (Heb. xii: 29), but it is a "refiner's fire" (Mal. iii: 2-3). It consumes the evil, and refines away the dross of error and sin. This corroborates the meaning we have shown to belong to the word expressive of the fire's duration. But whatever may be the purpose of the fire, it is not endless,— it is æonian. Benson [47] well says:—"The fire which consumed Sodom, etc., might be called eternal, as it burned until it utterly consumed them, beyond the possibility of their being inhabited or rebuilt. But the word will have a yet more emphatical meaning, if (as several authors affirm) that fire continued to burn a long while. If the fires burned but a short time, however, the example has lasted through the subsequent ages, or æons, and was therefore æonian, a continual warning." Albert Barnes, in his notes, gives the exact view, "The destruc-

---

[47] Paige's Com., Vol. VI., p. 368.

tion was as entire and perpetual as if the fires had been always
burning." The fact that Sodom and Gomorrah "are set forth,"
shows that the example is in this world. The fire, the destruction, the example, the vengeance, are all in this world; hence
they are said to be set forth. Besides, in the account of the
destruction of these cities, recorded in Genesis, not a word is
said of any fire or punishment beyond the present life. The
apostle appeals to the fate of those cities as a perpetual example. This is the utmost of his meaning. Canon Farrar[48] says,
"The expression 'quenchless fire,'—for the phrase 'that never
shall be quenched' is a simple mistranslation—is taken from
Is. lxvi: 24, and is purely a figure of speech, as it is there, or
as it is in Homer's Iliad, xvi: 123." In his appendix to the
volume he observes, "It was in answer to the bitter taunt of
Celsus, that the God of the Christians kindled a fire in which
all except Christians should be burned, that Origen first
argued that the fire should possess a purifying quality (*kathar-
sion*) for all those who had in themselves any materials for it
to consume." In fact, in Mark ix: 43, the word "never" in the
sentence "never shall be quenched," is added without warrant,
by the translators. The word *asbestos* ($\dot{\alpha}\sigma\beta\epsilon\sigma\tau o\nu$) is as correctly
rendered unquenched as unquenchable, and in either case
the word is used, as when we say of a conflagration it burned
unquenchably, meaning that it could not be put out till it
had spent its fury. Says Dr. Whiton in "Is Eternal Punishment Endless" (p. 19):—"Dr. Hodge, in his 'System of Theology' (iii: 877), well exemplifies the ease with which an assumed
meaning can be read into Scripture. He says, 'It is to be
remembered that, admitting the word everlasting to be ever
so ambiguous, the Bible says that the worm never dies, and
the fire is never quenched. We have, therefore, the direct assertion of the word of God that the sufferings of the lost are
unending.' A more unfounded statement could hardly be made.
To illustrate this, let us suppose the correctness of the doubtful statements that in the valley of Hinnom (Hebrew,

---

[48] Eternal Hope, Consequences of Sin.

Gehenna) the worm-breeding offal and filth of Jerusalem were consumed by ever-burning fires. It is certain that to such a place (whether a real or an imaginary place makes no difference) the words, 'where their worm dieth not and the fire is not quenched' (Mark ix: 48), could be applied with literal correctness. But no one would find the idea of absolute endlessness in such an expression. How, then, could Dr. Hodge find in the expression as figuratively used, a 'direct assertion' of endlessness which is not in the expression as literally used, unless he should import it furtively from his imagination, or some more reliable extraneous source? Such text-stuffing is as much of a fraud in its way, however unconscious, as ballot-stuffing."

II. Thess. i: 9, "Who shall be punished with everlasting destruction from the presence of the Lord, and from the glory of his power." Everlasting destruction ($\delta\lambda\epsilon\theta\rho\text{ov} \ \alpha\iota\acute{\omega}\nu\text{iov}$), does not signify remediless ruin, but long banishment from God's presence. This is what sin does for the soul. *Olethros* is not annihilation, but desolation. It is found but four times in the New Testament,—I. Thess. v: 3; I. Cor. v: 5; I. Tim. vi: 9. The passage in I. Cor. shows us how it is used: "Deliver such a one unto Satan for the destruction of the flesh, that the spirit may be saved in the day of the Lord Jesus." The destruction here is not final—it is conditional to the saving of the spirit. Everlasting destruction is equivalent to prolonged desolation.

II. Pet. ii: 17, "These are wells without water, clouds that are carried with a tempest; to whom the mist of darkness is reserved forever." Jude 13, "Raging waves of the sea, foaming out their own shame; wandering stars, to whom is reserved the blackness of darkness forever." "To whom is always reserved the blackness of darkness," would be a correct paraphrase of this language. Those referred to are like trees that bear no fruit, clouds that yield no water, foaming waves, stars that give no light. Endless duration was not thought of by Peter

or Jude. Indefinite duration, ages, is the utmost meaning of
eis aiōna, which is spurious in II. Pet. ii: 17, but genuine in
Jude 13.· The literal meaning is, "for an age." Eternity cannot
be extorted from the phrase.

Heb. vi: 2, "The doctrine of the æonian (*aiōnion*) judgment." We make no special explanation of this passage.
Whether the judgment of that age or the age to come, the
Christian, is meant, matters not. "The judgment of the age"
is the full force of the phrase *aiōnion* judgment.

An illuminating side-light is thrown on this subject by
commentators on I. Pet. iii: 18-20, in which Christ is said to
have "preached unto the spirits in prison." Alford says our
Lord "did preach salvation in fact, to the disembodied spirits,"
etc. Tayler Lewis:[49]—"There was a work of Christ in Hades;
he makes proclamation (ἐκήρυξεν) in Hades to those who are there
in ward. This interpretation, which was almost universally
adopted by the early Christian church," etc. Prof. Huidekoper:[50]—"In the second and third centuries every branch and
division of Christians believed that Christ preached to the
departed." Dictelmair[51] says this doctrine "*in omni coetu
Christiano creditum.*" Why preach salvation to souls whose
doom was fixed for eternity? And how could Christians
believe in that doctrine and at the same time give the æonian
words the meaning of eternal duration?

It is a pity that the noun (*aiōn*) has not always been rendered by the English word eon, or æon, and the adjective by
eonian or æonian; then all confusion would have been avoided.
Webster's Unabridged defines it as meaning a space or period
of time, an era, epoch, dispensation, or cycle, etc. He also
gives it the sense of eternity, but no one could have misunder-

---

49 Lange, on Ecclesiastes.
50 Mission to the Underworld, pp. 51-22.
51 Historia Dogmatis de Descensu Christi ad Inferos. Chs. iv-vi.

stood, had it been rendered æon. Suppose our translation read, "What shall be the sign of thy coming and of the end of the æon?" "The smoke of their torment shall ascend for æons of æons." "These shall go away into æonian chastisement," etc. The idea of eternity would not be found in the noun, nor of endless duration in the adjective, and the New Testament would be read as its authors intended.

The last resort of theologians has been to insist that the noun preceded by the preposition *eis* denotes absolute eternity, and that the phrase *eis ton aiōna*,[52] in the New Testament, must be so understood. In the Chicago discussion in the *Times* and *Inter-Ocean* of that city, in which the author of this volume maintained the negative, and Prof. J. R. Boise, D. D., Rev. Galusha Anderson, D. D., and Rev. G. R. Noyes, D. D., the affirmative, this point was made and strenuously insisted on from these passages :—Rev. xiv: 11, "And the smoke of their torment ascendeth up *forever and ever* (for æons of æons), and they have no rest *day nor night*, who worship the beast and his image, and whosoever receiveth the mark of his name." Xix: 3, "And her (Babylon's) smoke rose up *for ever and ever*" (for the æons of the æons). Xx: 10, "And the devil that deceived them was cast into the lake of fire and brimstone, where the beast and the false prophet are, and shall be tormented day and night *forever and ever*" (for the æons of the æons). It is said that these reduplications, if no other forms of the word, convey the idea of eternity. But the literal meaning of *eis aiōnas aiōnōn* (εἰς αἰῶνας αἰώνων) in the first text above, is ages of ages, and of *eis tous aiōnas tōn aiōnōn* (εἰς τοὺς αἰῶνας τῶν αἰώνων) in the other two, is the ages of the ages. It is thus rendered in the "Emphatic Diaglot." It is perfectly manifest to the commonest mind that if one age is limited, no number can be unlimited. Ages of ages is an intense expression of long duration, and if the word *aiōn* should be rendered eternity, "eternities of eternities" ought to be the translation, an expres-

---

[52] εἰς τὸν αἰῶνα.

sion too absurd to require comment. If *aiōn* means eternity,
any number of reduplications would weaken it. But while
ages of ages is proper enough, eternity of eternities would be
ridiculous.   On this phraseology Sir Isaac Newton [53] says,
"The ascending of the smoke of any burning thing *forever
and ever*, is put for the continuation of a conquered people
under the misery of perpetual subjection and slavery."   The
thought of eternal duration was not in the mind of Jesus or
his apostles in any of these texts, but long duration, to be
determined by the subject.

Aiōn governed by *eis* is limited in twenty-nine passages:
Matt. xxi : 19 ; Mark xi : 14 ; Luke i : 55 ; John iv : 14, vi : 51, 58, ix :
32, x : 28, xiii : 8, xiv : 16 ; I. Cor. viii : 13 ; Heb. v : 6, vi : 5, 20,
vii : 17, 21, etc.   In Heb. v : 6 our translation reads, "Thou art
a priest *forever*," but the literal is, "Thou art a priest for the
age," that is, the Christian age or dispensation.   In I. Cor.
viii : 13, Paul says he will "eat no meat while the world standeth" (*eis ton aiōna*), that is, while he lives.   Both these passages denote limited duration, as any reader can see.   So in
Luke i : 55, "As he spake to our fathers, to Abraham and to his
seed *forever*"—says our translation, but "of old" or "anciently"
is the real rendering.   The usage is the same in the New Testament as in the Old.   *Eis* governs *aiōn* in Ex. xxi : 6,—"The
servant was a slave *forever*" (*eis ton aiōna*), and yet all slaves
were set free every fifty years!   The same form is found in
Eccl. i : 4, and elsewhere.

Professor Boise declared in the Chicago secular press:
—"The strongest form of expression in the New Testament, in fact in the Greek language, ever used to denote
unending existence, is that combination of *aiōn* translated into
English, 'forever and ever.'   It is the phrase, *eis aiōnos
aiōnōn*, or *eis tous aiōnos tōn aiōnōn*.   I cannot conceive
of any word or any combination of words, in the Greek language,
or in any other language, which will convey the idea of eternal
duration in the future with more freedom from ambiguity and

[53] Daniel and Revelations, Lond. ed., 1733.

misconception, or with more solemn emphasis, than this one. If this phrase is inadequate, then every phrase is inadequate to the purpose. If this phrase is a failure, then all human language is a failure and a delusion. But we are not thus left without ideas, and words to convey them in; and of all languages, the Greek is acknowledged to be the most perspicuous. It is a remarkable fact, which every thoughtful man ought seriously to consider, that this phrase, translated 'forever and ever,' is predicated alike and without qualification of three ideas. These three ideas are, God's existence, the punishment of the wicked, and the happiness of the righteous. A few examples will suffice. 'To him that sitteth upon the throne, that liveth *forever and ever*' (*eis tous aiōnos tōn aiōnon*). 'They shall be tormented day and night *forever and ever*' (*eis tous aiōnas tōn aiōnōn*). They shall reign *forever and ever*' (*eis tous aiōnas tōn aiōnōn*). All these expressions are predicated in the New Testament of somebody. They assert the eternity of three things: of him who sitteth on the throne of torment day and night to somebody, of triumph and dominion to somebody. The eternity of the three things is affirmed in the same words. It would be easy to multiply examples like the foregoing."

Now, any careful reader must perceive that this is an example of the Hebraistic use of words in the Greek language. When the Jew wished to express a superlative thing, his only way was to duplicate the word. He still retained this habit in speaking Greek, and many instances of it occur in the New Testament. All that this "forever and ever" meansis a very great duration. In reference to this *dernier ressort*, we remark:

1. These phrases cannot be found, or anything resembling them, applied to sinners, more than twice in the whole New Testament. If they are vital, would they not be found over and over again, not only from Matthew, but from Genesis to Revelations?

2. Jesus never employs the language. Would he not repeat it over and over again, if it possesses the meaning claimed for it? And yet he entirely omits it.

3. Paul never describes the sinner's fate by the use of these terms. He "declared the whole counsel of God." Would he have omitted this phraseology if it unequivocally describes endless woe?

4. The only places in which it is found are in Jude once, and Revelations, toward the very end of that,– confessedly, the obscurest part of the Bible.

5. Even John uses it but once, and then he does not apply it to ordinary sinners, but to false worshipers. If the sinner's final torment is unanswerably taught by these words, would it not be repeatedly stated in the plainest parts of the Bible?

6. The same and similar terms are found in the Old Testament again and again. A brief glance at the Septuagint shows us the following:—*eis ton aiōna* is applied to less than fifty years of servitude, in Ex. xxi: 6; Lev. xxv: 46; Deut. xv: 17; to the smoke of Idumea, long since vanished, in Isa. xxxiv: 10; to Judah, Joel iii: 20; to the reign of a prince, in Ezek. xxxvii: 25; *eis aiōna aiōnos* is spoken of the stay of the righteous in the land, in Ps. xxxvii: 29; *eōs aiōnos* describes Abraham and his posterity in Luke i: 55; *eis ton aiōna tou aiōnas* refers to the official service of a priest, in Ps. cx: 4; and to a covenant, in Ps. cxi: 9; *eis kai eōs aiōnos* describes the time that the land was to be possessed, in Jer. vii: 7; and so does *ap aiōnos kai eōs aiōnos* in Jer. xxv: 5. And yet all these reduplications denote limited duration.

7. Thus, if the smoke of Idumea has ceased (Isa. xxxiv: 10), which was to be *eis ton aiōna* (for the age), why will not the smoke in Rev. xx: 10, which is *eis tous aiōnas tōn aiōnōn* (for the age of the ages)? "An age" is a certain length of time. "Ages of ages" is but a reduplication of age.

8. Orthodox critics never give their readers literal translations of the words. They conceal the real meaning of the sacred writers behind an exceedingly "free" rendering. "Forever" and "forever and ever," is the translation of theologians, and not of scholars.

9. If the word means eternity, reduplication is improper. To say "an eternal eternity," "an eternity of eternities,"

weakens and does not strengthen the solemn meaning of the word "eternity." But age can be thus strengthened by plurals and intensé reduplications. "An age of ages" is longer than "an age," but an "eternity of eternities" is nonsense.

10. The stereotyped argument is, that God, the saint's happiness and the sinner's misery, must be of the same duration, because the same Greek phrase describes each. Let us see how this will work with another word. We find the word "great" applied to evil, I. Sam. vi: 9; to earthly kings, Ps. cxxxvi: 17; to men, Nahum iii: 10; to merchants, Rev. xviii: 3; to the sea, John xv: 12; to a stone, Gen. xxix: 3; and to God, II. Sam. vii: 22; therefore kings, men, merchants, the sea, stones, and God, are all of the same size! This is not sound theology, good reasoning, nor common sense.

11. Such reasoning entirely ignores the Old Testament. Manifestly those for whom John intended the Apocalypse would understand these phrases just as they were used in the Old Testament. That meaning is limited duration.

12. Paul's declaration, I. Cor. viii: 13, "I will eat no meat" (eis ton aiōna), E. V., "while the world standeth," literally means, so long as I live. It has the same force as in Ex. xxi: 6, where the servant "shall serve his master (eis ton aiōna) 'forever,'" that is, till the year of jubilee only.

13. The language "day nor night," restricts the application of the language to this world.

14. If it requires eis to give aiōn the meaning of eternity, then aiōn of itself has no such meaning, so that every particle of stress that is placed on eis is removed from aiōnios and other forms of the word. The argument weakens the force of the word, on the whole, instead of strengthening it.

15. Dr. Whiton observes in "Is Eternal Punishment Endless," "The fact is, that the New Testament use of the phrase exactly corresponds to the Old Testament use of it in the LXX, where, as Dr. Tayler Lewis observes, 'immense extremes' occur 'in the use of the word.' He cites for comparison Ex. xxi: 6, the servant who does not wish to be freed 'shall serve

his master forever' (for the æon); and Deut. xxxii: 40, where
God says, 'I live forever' (for the æon). Here, temporal servitude and divine existence are comprehended within the elastic
limits of the same phrase. Compare John viii: 35, and xii:
34. In the English, also, we often use the word 'forever' with
exclusive reference to the present world,—precisely as the Scripture often employs *eis ton aiōna*—as, in legal phraseology, 'to
his heirs and assigns forever.' The result of a critical analysis
of all the passages where the phrase occurs is this: It uniformly denotes, not 'duration without end,' but permanent
duration,—permanent according to the nature of the subject,
covering in one case merely the period during which a blasted
fig-tree stands, and in another, the eternity of our Lord. To
affirm that it always implies duration without end, is as contrary to the fact as to affirm that it never does."

16. Dr. Robinson, in his New Testament Lexicon, seems to
be the authority for this opinion, which hangs eternity on a
preposition! If he is correct, the poet's words are indeed true:
"Great God, on what a slender thread, hang everlasting
things." But the very proofs Dr. Robinson cites, are against
him. He refers to the passages in Hebrews that speak of
Christ as a priest forever, forgetting that Christ's priesthood
is to end when he shall have accomplished his work. Hence,
Prof. Stuart declares,[54] " 'For the æon' is to be taken in a qualified sense here, as often elsewhere; *c. g.*, compare Luke i: 33,
with I. Cor. xv: 24-28. The priesthood of Christ will doubtless continue no longer than his mediatorial reign; for, when
his reign as mediator ceases, his whole work, both as mediator
and as priest, will have been accomplished."

Considering the connection, and all the circumstances, the
passages containing the preposition and the reduplications of
the word, are the weakest forms of the phraseology for the
advocates of the theory that it means endless. They are simple
multiplications of limited terms to denote long, but finite,
duration. And any student who will divest himself of

---

[54] Com. Heb., p. 340.

theological bias, and consult the words as a scholar, will agree with one of the greatest of England's theologians, Canon Farrar, who observes,[55] "It seems to me that if many passages of Scripture be taken quite literally, universal restoration is unequivocally taught, just as, if many passages be taken quite literally, the final annihilation of the wicked is taught; but that endless torments are nowhere clearly taught —the passages which appear to teach that doctrine being either obviously figurative or historically misunderstood. If the decision be made to turn solely on the literal meaning of Scripture, I have no hesitation whatever in declaring my strong conviction that the Universalist and Annihilist theories have far more evidence of this sort for them than the popular view."

To his testimony may be added that of one of Germany's greatest theologians, De Wette, who declares [56] that "the doctrine of eternal damnation cannot in any wise be retained, if we take the word eternal in a strict and absolute sense. For whatever is eternally damned must have been created in a state of eternal damnation, for eternity has no beginning."

Let the reader now recall the usage as we have presented it, and then reflect that all the forms of the word are applied to the punishment of human beings only fourteen times in the New Testatament, and ask himself the question, "Is it possible that so momentous a doctrine as this is only stated so small a number of times in divine revelation?" If it has the sense of limited duration, this is consistent enough, for then it will be classed with the other terms that describe the divine judgments. The fact that so many of those who speak or write never employ it at all, and that all of them together use it but fourteen times to qualify punishment, is a demonstration that he who has made known his will, and who would of all things have revealed so appalling a fate as endless woe, if he had it in preparation, has no such doom in store for immortal souls.

---

[55] Eternal Hope.   [56] Theolog. Zeitschrift, Zweites Heft, S. 120.

Let us now corroborate the conclusions we have reached, by consulting the Early Christians, who obtained their opinions from the apostles themselves, and who, of course, used these terms with their Bible meanings.

USAGE.—V.—*THE EARLY CHRISTIANS.*

The positions we have taken concerning the meaning of the æonian phraseology are corroborated and reënforced by Christian and other Greek writers in the early centuries of the church.   They derived the terms they employed directly from the apostles themselves, and used them as the apostles used them.   Certainly nothing can cast a backward illumination on the New Testament, and teach us the full meaning of our controverted words, as Jesus and the apostles understood them, so well as the language of the Christian Fathers and the Early Church.   We will therefore consult those who were perfectly familiar with the Greek tongue, and who passed the word along down the ages, from the apostles to their successors, for more than five hundred years.

Prof. Tayler Lewis,[1] in the course of learned disquisitions on the meaning of the olamic and æonian words of the Bible, refers to the oldest version of the New Testament, the Syriac, or the Peshito, and tells us how these words are rendered in this first form of the New Testament:—"So is it ever in the old Syriac version, where the one rendering is still more unmistakably clear.   These shall go into the pain of the *olam* (*aiŏn*, the world to come), and these to the life of the *olam*

----
[1] Lange's Excursus on Ecc. i: 3.

(*aiōn*, the world to come)." He refers to Matt. xix:16; Mark x:17; Luke xviii:18; John iii:15; Acts xiii:46; I. Tim. vi: 12, in which *aiōnios* is rendered belonging to *olam*, or world to come. *Eternal life*, the words in Matt. xxv:46, are rendered in the Peshito "the life of the world to come." Thus this eminent scholar, one of the best of modern critics, testifies that the earliest New Testament version did not give endless as the meaning of the word. Of Prof. Lewis, Dr. Beecher writes, [2] "We are not to suppose that so eminent an orthodox divine says these things in support of Universalism, a system which he decidedly and earnestly rejects."

The Apostles' Creed is the earliest Christian formula. The idea of endless torment is not hinted. "I believe in God, the Father Almighty; and in Jesus Christ, his only begotten Son, our Lord, who was born of the Virgin Mary by the Holy Ghost, was crucified under Pontius Pilate, buried, rose from the dead on the third day, ascended to the heavens, and sits on the right hand of the Father; whence he will come, to judge the living and the dead; and in the Holy Spirit; the holy church; the remission of sins; and the resurrection of the body."[3]

The New Testament was not compiled until A. D. 170, and the early church depended entirely on the Old Testament and tradition. Westcott says,[4] "The knowledge of the teachings of Christ and of the details of his life, to the close of the second century, were generally derived from tradition, and not from writings." Hence, as Beecher truly says,[5] "The account of the last judgment by Christ, and of the consequent retributions of eternal life, and eternal punishment . . is not referred to at all in the writings of the apostolic fathers, and is prominently brought forward for the first time in writing, in the latter part of the second century, by Justin Martyr and Irenæus."

"A comparison of the Nicene Creed with the Apostles'

---

[2] Hist. Fut. Ret.
[4] Intr. to Gos., p. 181.
[3] Murdoch's Mosheim, Vol. I., p. 96.
[5] Hist. Fut. Ret., p. 71.

Creed shows that æonian had the same force in ecclesiastical as in the inspired writings. The Apostles' Creed (at least as early as A. D. 200) confesses belief in "the æonian life" (English, "life everlasting"). The Niceno-Constantinopolitan Creed (A. D. 381) gives as the equivalent of this, "the life of the future æon" (English, "world to come"). Precisely thus the old Syriac Version (A. D. 100-150) rendered Matt. xxv: 46, "These shall go away to the pain of the *'olam,* and these to the life of the *'olam*" (or æon).[6]"

Our first reference to the patristic writers shall be to Ignatius,[7] who says the reward of piety "is incorruptibility and eternal life," "love incorruptible and perpetual life." Here the æonian life is strengthened by "incorruptible," showing that the word *aiōnion* alone was in his mind unequal to the task of expressing endless duration. He says, also, that Jesus "was manifested to the ages" (*tois aiōsin*). Of course, he intended to use no such ridiculous expression as "to the eternities."

The Sibylline Oracles (dated variously by different writers from 500 B. C. to 150 A. D.) teach æonian suffering and universal salvation beyond, showing how the word was then understood. The prophetess, who professed to write the Oracles, describes the saints as petitioning God for the salvation of the damned. Thus entreated, she says, "*God will deliver them* from the devouring fire and *aiōnion* gnashing of teeth." Restoration beyond æonian gnashing of teeth is here taught.

Justin Martyr[8] taught æonian suffering, and annihilation afterward. The wicked "are tormented as long as God wills that they should exist and be tormented.   .   . Souls both suffer punishment and die."[9] He uses the expression *eis ton aperanton aiōna.*[10] "The wicked undergo æonian punishment, and not for a thousand years, as Plato asserted." Here punishment is announced as limited. This

[6] Dr. Whiton's Is Eternal Puni hmen Endless? p. 72.
[7] A. D. 115.   [8] A. D. 140-202.
[9] Dialogue with Trypho, Chs. v, vi.   [10] Apol. Prim. cxxvii.

is evident from the fact that Justin Martyr taught the annihilation of the wicked: they are to be "tormented for the boundless æon," and then annihilated. His language is, "But I do not say, indeed, that all souls die; for that were certainly a piece of good fortune for the wicked. What, then? The souls of the pious remain in a better place, while those of the unjust and wicked are in a worse, waiting for the time of judgment. Thus, some who have appeared worthy of God never die; but others are punished *so long as God wills them to exist and be punished.*"

In the Orphica, referred to by Justin Martyr, occurs this passage, "Nor shall former things deprive you of dear life (φίλης αἰῶνος)." The date of these words is unknown, but Justin quotes them about A. D. 160, without explanation, so that they must have been intelligible then to ordinary readers. Hence, the literal meaning of "life" must have prevailed 160 years after Christ.

Irenæus [11] says, " The unjust shall be sent into inextinguishable and æōnian fire," and yet he taught that the wicked are to be annihilated.[12] "When it is necessary that the soul should no longer exist, the vital spirit leaves it, and the soul is no more, but returns thither whence it was taken." Dr. Beecher pertinently observes,[13] "What, then, are the facts as to Irenæus? Since he has been canonized as a saint, and since he stood in such close connection with Polycarp and with John, the apostle, there has been a very great reluctance to admit the real facts of the case. Massuetus has employed much sophistry in endeavoring to hide them. Nevertheless, as we shall clearly show hereafter, they are incontrovertibly these: that he taught a final restitution of all things to unity and order by the annihilation of all the finally impenitent. Express statements of his in his creed, and in a fragment referred to by Prof. Schaff, on universal restoration,[14] and in other parts of his great work

[11] Cont. Her. II, xxxiv.   [12] Ibid.
[13] Hist. Fut. Re:.   [14] Hist. Chr. Ch.

against the Gnostics, prove this beyond all possibility of refutation. The inference from this is plain. He did not understand *aiōnios* in the sense of eternal; but in the sense claimed by Prof. Lewis, that is, pertaining to the world to come." These are the words:—"Christ will do away with all evil, and make an end of all impurities." He further says [15] that certain persons "shall not receive from him (the Creator) length of days forever and ever." Thus the word denoted limited duration in his time, A. D. 170-200.

So Hermogenes,[16] who believed that all sinful beings will finally cease to be, must have understood Christ as applying *aiōnion* to punishment in the sense of limited duration, or he would not have believed in annihilation.

Titus of Bostra (340-370 A. D.) Dr. White informs us that he has discovered *aiōn* many times in "Against the Manicheans," by this father. Prof. Parker, of Lombard University, has translated several passages which follow. In the passage below marked 2, a free rendering is given of the preceding extract from section 27, that the meaning may be clear. In the paragraph marked 1 will be found the main passages, with the Greek words cited.

1. Titus says (section 18), "During the interval of the time (*aiōnos*) until now"; and in the same connection, "during periods (*aiōnas*) ten thousand times this"; and of a definite period he says, "It would be but a point of time, if it should be compared with the preceding boundless periods (*apeirois aiōsi*), for the former having a beginning and an end, has been completed, but the latter are altogether boundless, eternal (*aidioi*), and unbegotten." In section 27 he speaks of "so great a period" (*aiōna*), and in the same section says, "not for the shortest period of time (*aiōna*), but for one complete (*holon*) and boundless" (*apleton*). We give the whole context from section 27 in the next paragraph.

2. "Now, it is the more absurd, if God, wishing to rescue

15 Schaff, Vol. II., pp. 504, 573.
16 A. D. 260.

the earth from evil, has given it (the power of good) over to the outrage and destruction of its very essence by its remaining so long a time to dwell with what is bad, to share with it and to sin with it. That the essence of God should suffer this for at least one hour, or a point of time, so that it may be brought under subjection to what is bad, and may sin with it, would be the most absurd of all things." Again, speaking of the power of evil he says, "If its attack on the earth in respect to the disarrangement of matter is not to be endured, how much more is so great servitude and subjection of the nature of God unbearable? and not for the shortest *period of time*, but for one entire and boundless."

In these passages the adjectives are more than ever significant. Titus is careful to speak of a *whole* as well as a boundless αἰών, and calls it αἴδιος also. Nothing can better demonstrate the actual meaning of the term than such an employment of it.

Origen used the expressions "*aiōnion* fire" and "*aiōnion* punishment" to express his idea of the duration of punishment. Yet he believed that in all cases sin and suffering would cease and be followed by salvation. He was the most learned man of his time, and his example proves that *aiōnion* did not mean endless at the time he wrote (A. D. 200-253). Dr. Beecher says,[17] "As an introduction to his system of theology, he states certain great facts as a creed believed by all the church. In these he states the doctrine of future retribution as *aiōnion* life, and *aiōnion* punishment, using the words of Christ. Now, if Origen understood *aiōnion* as meaning strictly eternal, then to pursue such a course would involve him in gross and palpable self-contradiction. But no one can hide the facts of the case. After setting forth the creed of the church as already stated, including *aiōnion* punishment, he forthwith proceeds, with elaborate reasoning, again and again to prove the doctrine of universal restoration. The conclusion from these facts is obvious: Origen did not understand *aiōnios* as meaning eternal, but rather as meaning per-

---

[17] Hist. Fut. Ret., pp. 176-189.

taining to the world to come.   .   .   .   Two great
facts stand out on the page of ecclesiastical history.   One, that
the first system of Christian theology was composed and
issued by Origen in the year 230 after Christ, of which a fundamental and essential element was the doctrine of the universal restoration of all fallen beings to their original holiness
and union with God.   The second is, that after the lapse of a
little more than three centuries, in the year 544, this doctrine
was for the *first time condemned and anathematized* as
heretical.   This was done, not in the general council, but in a
local council called by the Patriarch Mennas, at Constantinople, by the order of Justinian.   During all this long interval,
the opinions of Origen and his various writings, were an element of power in the whole Christian world.   For a long time
he stood high, as the greatest luminary of the Christian world.
He gave an impulse to the leading spirits of subsequent ages
and was honored by them as their greatest benefactor.   At
last, after all his scholars were dead, in the remote age of Justinian, he was anathematized as a heretic of the worst kind.
The same also was done with respect to Theodore of Mopsuestia, of the Antiochian school, who held the doctrine of
universal restitution on a different basis.   This, too, was done
long after he was dead, in the year 553.   From and after this
point, the doctrine of future eternal punishment reigned with
undisputed sway during the middle ages that preceded the
Reformation.   What, then, was the state of facts, as to the
leading theological schools of the Christian world, in the age
of Origen, and some centuries after?   It was, in brief, this:
There were at least six theological schools in the Church at
large.   Of these six schools, one, and only one, was decidedly
and earnestly in favor of the doctrine of future eternal punishment.   One was in favor of the annihilation of the wicked.
Two were in favor of the doctrine of universal restoration
on the principles of Origen, and two in favor of universal restoration on the principles of Theodore of Mopsuestia.

   "It is also true that the prominent defenders of the doctrine
of universal restoration were decided believers in the divinity

of Christ, in the trinity, in the incarnation and atonement, and in the great Christian doctrine of regeneration; and were, in piety, devotion, Christian activity and missionary enterprise, as well as in learning and intellectual power and attainments, inferior to none in the best ages of the church, and were greatly superior to those by whom, in after ages, they were condemned and anathematized.

"It is also true that the arguments by which they defended their views were never fairly stated and answered. Indeed, they were never stated at all. They may admit of a thorough answer and refutation, but even if so, they were not condemned and anathematized on any such grounds, but simply in obedience to the arbitrary mandates of Justinian, whose final arguments were deposition and banishment for those who refused to do his will.

"Consider, now, who Theodore of Mopsuestia was, not as viewed by a slavish packed council, met to execute the will of a Byzantine despot, but by one of the most eminent evangelical scholars of Germany,—Dorner. Of him he says, 'Theodore of Mopsuestia was the crown and climax of the school of Antioch. The compass of his learning, his acuteness, and, as we must suppose, also, the force of his personal character, conjoined with his labors through many years, as a teacher both of churches and of young and talented disciples, and as a prolific writer, gained for him the title of Magister Orientis. He labored on uninterruptedly till his death, in the year 427, and was regarded with an appreciation the more widely extended as he was the first oriental theologian of his time.' " [18]

Mosheim says of Origen :—"Origen possessed every excellence that can adorn the Christian character; uncommon piety from his very childhood; astonishing devotedness to that most holy religion which he professed; unequaled perseverance in labors and toils for the advancement of the Christian cause; untiring zeal for the Church and for the extension of Christianity; an elevation of soul which placed him above all ordi-

---

[18] Doctrine of Person of Christ., Div. II., Vol. I., p. 50, Edinburgh.

nary desires or fears; a most permanent contempt of wealth, honor, pleasures, and of death itself; the purest trust in the Lord Jesus, for whose sake, when he was old and oppressed with ills of every kind, he patiently and perseveringly endured the severest sufferings. It is not strange, therefore, that he was held in so high estimation, both while he lived and after death. Certainly, if any man deserves to stand first in the catalogue of saints and martyrs, and to be annually held up as an example to Christians, this is the man, for, except the apostles of Jesus Christ and their companions, I know of no one, among all of those enrolled and honored as saints, who excelled him in virtue and holiness." [19]

Now, how could universal salvation have been the prevailing doctrine in that age of the church, unless the word applied to punishment in Matt. xxv: 46, was understood by such men as Origen and Theodore, as well as by other Christians, to mean limited duration?

Eusebius, the father of ecclesiastical history, who was a Universalist, says,[20] "If the subjection of the son to the father means union with him, then the subjection of *all* to the son means union with him." How could Eusebius be a Universalist, and regard *aiōnios* as meaning endless? And how could he describe the darkness preceding creation thus:[21]—"These for a long time had no limit," they continued "for a long æon" (*dia polun aiōna*). To say that the darkness that ended with the creation, endured for a long eternity, would be absurd enough.

The fact that Origen and others taught æonian punishment after death, and salvation beyond it, demonstrates that in Origen's time the word had not the meaning of endless, but did mean at that date, indefinite or limited duration. Also, the consideration that those who opposed the Universalist fathers never quoted *aiōnios* against them, is conclusive evi-

---

[19] Hist. Com. on Christ. before Const ntine, Vol. II., p. 149.
[20] De Ecc. Theol. (in Migne) VI., p. 1030, on I. Cor. xv: 28.
[21] Hist., Vol. I., p. 173.

dence that they did not attach the idea of endlessness to the word.

Readers curious to look up the state of opinion during the centuries following the age of Origen, can refer to the authorities cited below.[22]

Somewhere about a century after the death of John, appeared a strange book, evidently written as a fiction, which sets forth the views current at the time, namely, "The Gospel of Nicodemus." It describes the ministry of Christ in Hades. In part II., chapter 8, it declares that when Jesus arrived at Hades, the gates burst open, and taking Adam by the hand, Jesus said, "Come all with me, as many as have died through the tree which he touched, for behold I raise you all up through the tree of the cross." This book shows conclusively that the Christians of that date did not regard æonian punishment as interminable, inasmuch as those who were sentenced to that condition, were sometimes, at least, released.

Gregory Nyssen[23] proves that the word had the meaning of limited duration in his day. He says,[24] "Whoever considers the divine power will plainly perceive that it is able at length to restore by means of the *aiōnion* purgation and expiatory sufferings, those who have gone even to this extremity of wickedness." Thus everlasting punishment and salvation beyond were taught in the fourth century.

Augustine[25] was the first known to argue that *aiōnios* signified endless. He at first maintained that it always meant thus, but at length abandoned that ground, and only claimed that it had that meaning sometimes. He "was very imperfectly acquainted with the Greek language." [26]

---

[22] Assemanni Bib. Orient., Vol. I., Part i, pp. 223-4, 324.—Döderlein, Inst. Theol. Christ., Vol. II., pp. 200-1.—Jacobi, Bohn's edition.—Neander's Hist. Christian Dogmas.—Guericke, Shedd's translation, pp. 308-340.—Neander, Torrey's translation, Vol. II., p. 251-2.—Dorner's Hist. Person of Christ., Vol. II., pp. 28, 30, 50.—Dr. Schaff, Hist. Christ. Ch., Vol. II., pp. 731 504.—Gieseler, Vol. I., p. 370.—Kurtz, Text Book Christ. Hist., p. 137-202.—Hagenbach, quoting from Augustine Civitate Dei, Liber. XXI., C ap. xvi.

[23] A. D. 370-3.   [24] De Infantibus, p. 174.

[25] A. D. 430.   [26] Ancient Hist. Univ.—See his Confession.

A. D. 410 Avitus brought to Spain, from Jerome, in Palestine, a translation of Origen, and taught that punishments are not endless; for "though they are called *aiŏnion*, yet that word in the original Greek does not, according to its etymology and frequent use, signify endless, but refers only to the duration of the age." [27]

President White refers us to the end of the fourth book of Manetho's "Influence of the Stars." "These principles (or laws) of the heavenly bodies have been created (or formed) by which past and present and future time are measured (literally, have been measured) by *immense* periods (εκμέτροις αιῶσι), and this will continue *unto* or into the ages (εις αιῶνας)." Now, the latter expression might be rendered "for ever," but the context, it would seem, hardly admits of it, for the "principles or laws through which the past has been measured by *measureless œons,*" were *created,* i. e., had a *beginning,* and as the idea of absolute eternity cannot obtain with regard to the past, neither can it obtain with respect to the future.

Manetho lived in the third century B. C., but this treatise "On the Influence of the Stars," attributed to him, was actually written in the fifth century of the Christian era.

Near the beginning of the sixth book the following passage occurs:—"The wisest Homer has spoken of the generations of men which the boundless age has produced," (literally, fitted or joined together). Boundless or immense age is μυρίος αιών—μυρίος is applied to a number indefinitely great. These passages are especially instructive because of the adjective joined to the word αιών.

In fact, every Universalist and every Annihilationist among the fathers of the early church is a standing witness testifying that the word was understood as we claim, in their day. Believers in the Bible, accepting its utterances as implicit truth, how could they be Universalists or Annihilationists with the Greek Bible before them, and *aiŏnion* punishment taught there, unless they give to the word thus used the meaning of

---

[27] Hieronymi Epist.

limited duration? Accordingly, besides those alluded to above, we appeal to those ancient Universalists, the Basilidians (A. D. 130), the Carpocratians (A. D. 140), Clemens Alexandrinus (A. D. 190), Gregory Thaumaturgus (A. D. 220-50), Ambrose (A. D. 250), Didymus the Blind (A. D. 350-90), Diodore of Tarsus (A. D. 370-90), Isidore of Alexandria (A. D. 370-400), Jerome (A. D. 380-410), Palladius of Gallatia (A. D. 400), and others, not one of whom could have been a Universalist unless he ascribed to this word the sense of limited duration. To most of them Greek was as familiar as English is to us.

The Emperor Justinian,[28] in calling the celebrated local council which assembled in 544, addressed his edict to Mennas, Patriarch of Constantinople, and elaborately argued against the doctrines he had determined should be condemned. He does not say, in defining the Catholic doctrine at that time, "We believe in *aiōnion* punishment," for that was just what the Universalist, Origen himself, taught. Nor does he say, "The word *aiōnion* has been misunderstood; it denotes endless duration," as he would have said had there been such a disagreement. But, writing in Greek, with all the words of that language from which to choose, he says, "The holy church of Christ teaches an endless *aiōnios* (*ateleutetos aiōnios*) life to the righteous, and endless (*ateleutetos*) punishment to the wicked." *Aiōnios* was not enough in his judgment to denote endless duration, and he employed *ateleutetos*, the word of all others in the copious Greek tongue that expressed endless duration. Now, if *aiōnios* then meant endless duration, why did he qualify it by *ateleutetos*? The fact that he did, demonstrates that even as late as A. D. 540, *aiōnios* meant limited duration, and required an added word to impart to it the force of endless duration.

Olympiodorus, an Aristotelian philosopher, contemporary with Justinian, is quoted by Dr. Edward Beecher[29] as saying, "When *aiōnios* is used in reference to a period which, by

---

assumption, is infinite and unbounded, it means eternal, but when used in reference to times or things limited, the sense is limited to them." He denies that punishment is endless, but says that it is *aiōnion*, that is, lasting for a definite *aiōn*, after which the sinner is purged. Dr. Beecher quotes, through Prof. Abbott, of Cambridge, Mass., from Ideler's edition of the commentary of Olympiodorus on the "Meteorologica of Aristotle"[30] the following from Olympiodorus :--"Do not suppose the soul is punished for endless aions[31] in Tartarus. Very properly the soul is not punished to gratify the revenge of the divinity, but for the sake of healing. But we say that the soul is punished for an aionian period,[32] calling its life, and its allotted period of punishment, its[33] *aiōn*."[34] Undeniably, endless æons are here contrasted with an æonian period, the former denoting endless, and the latter limited, duration. If *aiōn* means eternity, why endless *aiōns?*

Now, Ignatius, Polycarp, Hermas, Justin Martyr, Irenœus, Hyppolytus, Justinian, and others (from A. D. 115 to A. D. 544), use the word *aiōnion* to define punishment. And yet some of these taught that decay out of conscious existence is the natural tendency of men, from which only some are saved by God's grace. Previous to this decay, or extinction of being, they held that men experience *aiōnion* punishment. It is not endless, for it ceases. Justin Martyr says, "Souls suffer *aiōnion* punishment and die." The punishment is in the future world, but it concludes with extinction, he says, and yet it is *aiōnion*.

Canon Farrar says,[35] "Even Augustine admits (what, indeed, no one can deny,) that in Scripture *aiōn*, *aiōnios* must in many instances mean 'having an end,' and St. Gregory of Nyssa, who at least knew Greek, uses *aiōnios* as the epithet of 'an interval.'" [See appendix D.]

---

[30] Vol. I., p. 282, f. 32., Aldine ed., Olymp., quoted by Dr. Beecher, Hist. Fut. Ret., note 4.

[31] 'Απείρους αἰῶνας.   [32] 'Αἰώνιως

[33] 'Αἰών.   [34] Hist. Fut. Ret., p. 166.

[35] Excursus on *Aiōnios*, in Eternal Hope.

These eminent patristic writers and early Christians, and others, demonstrate by their use of the word that it did not mean endless duration for at least six centuries after Christ. To say that any one who contradicts them is correct, and that they did not know the meaning of the word, or use it correctly, is like saying that an Australian, twelve hundred years hence, will be better able to give an accurate definition of English words in common use to-day, than we are ourselves. They could not be mistaken, and the fact that they required qualifying words to give *aiōnion* the sense of endless duration—that they used it to describe punishment when they believed in the annihilation of the wicked, or in their restoration subsequent to *aiōnion* punishment, irrefragably demonstrates that the word had not the meaning of endless to them, and if not to them, then it must have been utterly destitute of it.

There are few things in the history of language more astounding than that this word should have been so obscured by error and ignorance, as to carry a meaning for centuries utterly foreign and alien. It has resembled those frightful daubs which monkish superstition has wrought, which, when cleansed by the hand of taste, are seen to have been palimpsests, and that under the crude design of the monk are concealed the rare achievements of genius. It is the work of modern scholarship to restore the word to the meaning it had for a thousand years before, and at least five hundred years after, Christ. Certainly the Christian Fathers employed it as it was used by the ancient Greeks, the LXX, and the New Testament authors, and it is the duty of the Christian to-day to understand it as did all who used it until less than fifteen hundred years ago. Even the German Lutheran, J. C. Dœderlein, admits.[36]—"As to public teaching, the most ancient testimony against the end of future punishment is extant in a canon of Justinian's tractate to Mennas against

---

[36] Instit. Theol., Chr. II., pp. 199-2

Origen (ap. Harduin. vol. iii. Concil. p. 279, can. 9):—'If any one says or holds that the punishment of demons and impious men is temporary, and that it will have an end at some time, that is to say, that there is a restoration of demons or impious men, he is accursed.' It is also evident that very many doctors held the same view. . . . But that was not the confession of all, and the more highly distinguished in Christian antiquity any one was for learning, so much the more did he cherish and defend the hope of future torments some time ending.[37] This, however, was not the view of a few persons, and one privately entertained, but general, and maintained by many advocates. Augustine, at least (Enchiridion, c. 112), testifies that 'some, nay, very many, pity with human feeling the everlasting punishment of the damned, and do not believe that it is to be so.' . . The following age, although a belief in perpetual torments prevailed by authority, yet clearly did not lack milder views."

Should any reader of this volume ask, "Why all this labor to establish the meaning of one word?" the author would answer that such a labor should seem unnecessary. Men ought to refuse to credit such a doctrine as that of endless punishment on higher grounds than those of verbal definition. Reverence, not to say respect, for God, the fact that he is the Father of mankind, should compel all to reject the doctrine of endless torment, though the weight of argument were a thousand-fold to one in favor of the popular definition of this word. But there are those who disregard the moral argument against the doctrine which is unanswerable; who violate the noblest instincts of the heart and soul, which plead trumpet-tongued against that horrible nightmare of doubt and unbelief; who cling to the mere letter of the word, which kills, and ignore the spirit, which gives life; who insist that all the voices of reason and sentiment should be disregarded because the Bible declares the doctrine of endless punishment for sinners. It is

---

[37] See motto on title page.

for such that these facts have been gathered, and this essay written, that no shred nor vestige even of verbal probability should exist to mislead the mind, and so seem to sanction the doctrine that defames God and distresses man; that it might be seen that the letter and the spirit of the word agree, and are in perfect accord with the dictates of reason, the instincts of the heart, and the impulses of the soul, in rejecting the worst error that ever yet was invented,—the monstrous falsehood that represents God as consigning the souls he has created in his own image to interminable torment. It is because the word under examination is the foundation-stone of that evil structure, that this monograph has been written.

The author believes it has appeared as the result of this discussion that

1. There is nothing in the etymology of the word warranting the erroneous interpretation of it.

2. That the definitions of lexicographers uniformly given not only allow but compel the view we have advocated.

3. That Greek writers before and at the time the Septuagint was made, always gave the word the sense of limited duration.

4. That such is the general usage in the Old Testament.

5. That the Jewish Greek writers at the time of Christ ascribed to it limited duration.

6. That the New Testament thus employs it.

7. That the usage for several centuries after Christ was uniform with the ten centuries before Christ.

Hence it follows that the readers of the Bible are under the most imperative obligations to understand the word in all cases as denoting limited duration, unless the subject treated, or other qualifying words, compel them to understand it differently.

If our positions are well taken, the Bible does not teach the doctrine of endless torment; for, it will be admitted, that if this word does not teach it, then that dreadful dogma cannot be found in the sacred pages.

11

Can any evidence on any subject be more unanswerable
than the foregoing? Any one department of the proof we have
adduced would seem sufficient to sustain our position, but each
has a cumulative force, and all together are irrefragable. Each
one of the multitude of facts we give is as a fiber, in a cable whose
strength no power can break, and we close our argument, con-
fidently affirming that the voice of Greek literature for a
millennium and a half declares that limited duration is the
utmost force of the æonian phraseology.

APPENDIX A.

We are informed by President White, who has made this subject a patient and conscientious study for years, that many passages might be quoted from the Greek Anthology to the same purport as those we have taken from the Classics. We here cite passages which he has found.

The first is a remarkable extract from Xenophon (fifth century B. C.). Its value on this question can hardly be over-estimated. It is found in the tenth Chap. of the Agesilaus, and the fourth section. "Having reached the extreme limit of HUMAN LIFE" (ἀνθροπίνου αἰῶνος). Here we have a *human* (ἀνθροπίνου) *aion*. It means the period of a human life. Does not this more than suggest that the length of the *aion* depends upon that to which it is applied?

The most striking passage, perhaps, to be found in Greek literature, contains the three words βιος, αιων and ἀΐδιος. It is found in the concluding paragraph of the Agesilaus. Xenophon is highly eulogising his hero, and continues thus :—"Who in the vigor of life, inspired his enemies with such fear as did Agesilaus even when he had already reached the longest *period of life* (αἰῶνος) allotted to man? Whom would his enemies prefer to have out of the way more than Agesilaus even when he was in extreme old age? Who infused such confidence into his allies as did Agesilaus, and that, too, when he was already on the very verge of life (βίον)? What youth was more cherished by friends than was Agesilaus, though dying, well stricken in years? Thus, in fine, did this man continue to be useful to his country, and while still, even to the end of his career, rendering signal service to his city, he was brought to his *eternal home,* (ἀΐδιον οἴκησιν); having erected monuments of his valor throughout the whole earth, but having the good fortune to obtain a royal tomb in his native country." Here the idea of existence (*aion*), of life itself (*bios*), and of eternity (*aidion*), are all contained in one passage, and the fact that *aion* denotes a limited period, and *aidion* an unlimited could hardly be stated in plainer terms.

The same idea is distinctly taught in a passage from the *Argonautica* of Apollonius Rhodius (B. C. 200.), "For a period of *time* (αἰῶν) sufficiently long has already elapsed." (Argonautica, line 276.) The time of this author is between the time of the Septuagint translation and that of Christ.

In the Anthologica Græca (ed. Jacobs), Vol. II, p. 794, is an epigram upon a work of Apollodorus (Mythologus), entitled "The Bibliotheca." Apollodorus lived about 140 B. C. This epigram, therefore, could hardly have been written earlier than 100 B. C. It reads thus:—"Drawing out the *coil of time* (Αἰῶνος σπείρημα)." In another epigram, found on p. 795, of the same volume, occurs the following passage:—"(Dexippus) who, having considered well the long history of time (αἰῶνος), faithfully related it." As the Dexippus here spoken of lived in the third century after Christ, we may fix the probable date of this epigram at A. D. 300.

One more citation must suffice. Arethas, a Christian Bishop (A. D. 540?), in some verses written on the death of his sister, says, "Swift fate (death) has extinguished the *lamp of my life* (αἰῶνος)."

APPENDIX B.

There is but one Greek word besides *aiōnios* rendered everlasting, and applied to punishment, in the New Testament, and that is the word *aïdios*, found in Jude 6:—"And the angels which kept not their first estate, but left their own habitation, he hath reserved in *everlasting* (ἀΐδιος) chains under darkness, unto the judgment of the great day." This word is found in but one other place in the New Testament, viz., Rom. i: 20, "For the invisible things of him from the creation of the world are clearly seen, being understood by the things that are made, even his *eternal* power and Godhead."

Now, it is admitted that this word, among the Greeks, had the sense of eternal, and should be understood as having that meaning wherever found, unless by express limitation it is shorn of its proper meaning. It is further admitted that had *aïdios* occurred where *aiōnios* does, there would be no escape from the conclusion that the Greek Classics, and the Old and New Testaments, teach endless punishment. It is further admitted that the word is here used in the exact sense of *aiōnios*, as is seen in the succeeding verse:—"Even as Sodom and Gomorrah, and the cities about them in like manner, giving themselves over to fornication, and going after strange flesh, are set forth for an example, suffering the vengeance of *eternal* fire." That is to say, the "*aïdios* chains" in verse 6 are "*even as*" durable as the "*aiōnian* fire" in verse 7. No less and no more durable. Which word modifies the other?

1. The construction of the language shows that the latter word limits the former. The *aïdios* chains are even as, equal to, the *aiōnion* fire. As if one should say, "I have been infinitely troubled, I have been vexed for an hour"; or, "He is an endless talker, he can talk five hours on a stretch." Now, while "infinitely" and "endless" convey the sense of unlimited, they are both limited by what follows, as *aïdios*, eternal, is in this instance limited by *aiōnios*, indefinitely long.

2. That this is the correct exegesis is evident from still another limitation of the word. "The angels . . . he hath reserved in *aïdios* chains UNTO the judgment of the great day." Had Jude said that the angels are held in *aïdios* chains, and stopped there, not limiting the word, we should not dare deny that he taught *their* eternal imprisonment. But when he limits the duration by *aiōnion* and then expressly states that it is only *unto* a certain date, we understand that the imprisonment will terminate, even though we find applied to it a word that intrinsically signifies eternal duration, and that was used by the Greeks to convey the idea of eternity, and was attached to punishment by the Greek Jews of our Savior's times, to describe endless punishment, in which they were believers.

But observe that, while this word, *aïdios*, was in universal use among the Greek Jews of our Savior's day, to convey the idea of eternal duration, and was used by them and the heathen to teach endless punishment, he never allowed himself to use it in connection with punishment, nor did any of his disciples but one, and he but once, and then he carefully and expressly limited its meaning, and did not apply it to human misery but to fallen angels. Can demonstration go further than this to show that Jesus carefully avoided the phraseology by which his contemporaries described the doctrine of endless punishment? He never employed it. What ground, then, is there for saying that he adopted the language of his day on this subject? Their language was *aïdios timoria*, endless torment. His language was *aiōnion kolasin*, age-lasting correction. They described unending ruin, he, discipline, resulting in reformation.

Dr. Whiton most pertinently observes:*—"If now it be assumed that *aïdian* regularly denotes that which is strictly everlasting, then we are met by a question that ought to be answered, 'Why, with this word at hand, to give precise expression to the idea of endless duration, have the sacred books never employed it with reference to the future of the human race, but always the indeterminate word *æonian?*' For instance, in the very next verse (7), Jude, in speaking of the pun-

* Is Eternal Punishment Endless? pp. 27-28.

ishment of Sodom and Gomorrah, drops the word *aidian*, just used with reference to the angels, and takes the word *æonian*, a change scarcely noticed in our version by the change of 'everlasting' to 'eternal.' *Æonian* and *aidian* may be used interchangeably in the writings of Plato, but they are not in the writings of the Apostles; in these the futurity of mankind is only *æonian*.

"Professor Bartlett pronounces the occurrence of *aidion* here (in evidence, as he assumes, that *æonian* is the same as *endless*) to be 'singular and startling.' His wonder suggests to us a further wonder. If *aidian* has the meaning of endlessness any more clearly and strictly than *æonian*, then the entire avoidance of this clearer and stricter term throughout the New Testament as descriptive of human destiny in the future state is certainly very 'singular,' even if not actually startling.

"It might, however, be regarded as even 'startling,' if, after all the reliance that has been placed upon this passage, it should turn out that a limited interpretation is here attached to *aidian* by its context. What if Jude only meant to affirm that the imprisonment of the fallen angels is 'everlasting' until the Judgment!—thus leaving the after ages unspoken of?"

Thus the word whose meaning of endlessness no one disputes, is

1. Never employed to denote the perpetuity of human suffering.

2. It is not applied to the fate of man at all, but only to certain "angels."

3. When applied to fallen angels it is expressly limited by being stated to be even as "*æonian*," no more.

4. It ends at the judgment, being only "until" then.

5. Finally, with this word right within reach, Jesus and his Apostles declined to use it to describe the punishment of the sinner, but only employed the *æonian* terms, which uniformly possess the sense of limited duration. Can such an omission be explained except on the ground that he taught a limited punishment?

Many instructive passages illustrating the use of αἴδιος may be found in the work of Gregory of Nyssa entitled, "Against Eunomius." In the "Summary" of the work I find the following passage:—"The Creator of the world had no beginning, but is *without beginning and eternal* (αἴδιος)." Again he says, "Christ is the good will of the Father which was from *eternity* (ἐξ αἰδίου)." Wishing to make clear his view of the eternity of God, Gregory says, (Vol. I., p. 156 Oehler's ed.), "We affirm concerning the eternity (ἀϊδιότητος) of God what we have heard from prophecy, that God is (was) *before time* (προαιώνιος), and *rules time* (αἰῶνα), and (literally) *unto time* (ἐπ' αἰῶνα), and *beyond* (ἔτι)." "For this reason" he continues, "we pronounce (define) him to be before all beginning and beyond all end." Again, p. 377 of t:e same volume, Gregory says, "But the creation has a beginning *in time* (*αἰῶνας*), but what beginning think you had the *maker* (*ποιητοῦ*) of the ages (*τῶν αἰώνων*)? Similar passages, however, by this writer are too numerous for exhaustive citation. More than one hundred to the same import might be collated from his works. Gregory flourished A. D. 370.

The reader of the Fathers will see that they made a wide and clear distinction between *aïdios* and *aiōn*. [President White has furnished the last two paragraphs.]

APPENDIX C.

There is a seeming contradiction among authors as to the opinions of the Jews, at the time of Christ, concerning the duration of punishment. Josephus expressly declares that the Pharisees and Essenes regarded it as interminable (see p. 88), while the Rabbins and Jewish authors insist that the doctrine was never properly held by the Jews (p. 131). How shall the discrepancy be reconciled? Thus: though the Old Testament does not teach the doctrine (see pp. 86-7), and though it could not be legitimately held, yet at the time of Christ multitudes of the Jewish people, more particularly the learned classes, had become so Hellenized (pp. 62-63), and this false Pagan doctrine had obtained such a foothold that Jesus rebuked the Scribes and Pharisees for following the lead of tradition (Mark vii: 9,13 ; Matt. xxii: 29) instead of obeying the voice of Scripture. So thoroughly were they saturated with the errors of Paganism, on this point, when Jesus revealed the great fact of a resurrection to universal holiness and happiness (Mark xii, Luke xx) that "the people were astonished at his doctrine." Though not properly and legitimately a Jewish tenet. there can be no doubt that the Pharisees and their followers, and the Essenes and the Pagans, held to the doctrine, so that when Jesus spoke, many, at least, of his hearers, accepted it. These facts explain the conflicting statements of authors on this subject.

APPENDIX D.

The astonishing drift of theological criticism from all directions in the lines that Universalist scholarship has pursued for the last half century, is well illustrated in an able work that reaches us from England, just as our last pages are completed—"The Three-fold Basis of Universal Restitution." London: Williams and Norgate. The author says (pp. 128-30, 131-34):

Aionios is derived from *aion* (*aion* being a compound of *aie* always, and *on* being), and is commonly employed in Scripture to express a period or time of indefinite duration, not absolute, but relative perpetuity. Just in the same way as we use the terms eternity, perpetuity, when we speak of the region of eternal (perpetual) snow, the eternal ice of the poles, perpetual curacy. Thus *aion* is the literal Greek equivalent of the Hebrew term עוֹלָם (hidden time), *for ever*, *the world or universe*. The Bible has no distinct, separate expression for eternity in the absolute sense of infinite duration. All the Biblical expressions of duration imply or denote long periods connected with one another. "The formula εἰς τον αἰῶνα, *to eternity*, *for ever*, is in every respect parallel with the others, εἰς τοὺς αἰῶνας, *for ages*, *for ever*, εἰς τοὺς αἰῶνας τῶν αἰῶνων, *for ages of ages*, *for ever and ever* (Gal. i: 5), expressions which denote the aeternitas a parte post, or the future conceived as an indefinitely extended period."* In such expressions as "before all ages," "before the world," the true meaning of *aion* as denoting, not absolute eternity, but duration, conceived as an indefinitely extended period' or periods, is manifest. As derived from *aion*, signifying age or dispensation, *aionios* may be properly rendered age-long or age-enduring. It is true, that *aion*, as derived from *aie* and *on*, might in virtue of its abverbial component *aie*, always, be employed to denote that which is absolutely eternal. We do not, however, find that it is so used in the Scriptures. It is frequently employed in the New Testament, in the sense of age or dispensation, and is the term used by our Lord to designate "the contrasted epochs of Judaism and Christianity." Hence, *aionios* is the adjective form of *aion*, and as applied to the same dispensations or epochs, is fitly rendered age-long. Thus the idea that *aionios* as applied to rewards and punishments means endless, has no foundation in the literal sense of the term, nor in its scriptural and general applications. There are, however, insuperable objections against this sense being given to the term in the case of punishments. Not on grounds of philology alone must its meaning in this instance be decided, but on other grounds as well. The state of punishment under God's moral government cannot, in the nature of things, be endless or final. The end for which punishment exists requires that it should cease. Men were created not to suffer endless misery, but to be made perfect and happy. Punishment exists not as an absolute end, but a means. It is necessary, to the moral training of man, that the evil into which he is betrayed should be manifested in its appropriate fruit, its essential misery and falsity; and for this end punishment is inflicted. When the lesson has been learned, and the evil way is renounced, punishment must cease. To say that God wills punishment to exist for ever, is to affirm that God fatally dooms some men to evil. It is to hold that through eternity God preserves existence to a

---

*Olshausen on the Gospels (Matt. xii: 31, 22).

personal being, only in order to take from him, through eternity, the possibility of being good or ceasing to do evil.

While we have no clear proof that the term *aionios* is ever used in Scripture in the sense of absolute eternity, we have abundant evidence that it is often used in a sense that does not involve that idea. On this ground, as well as on grounds of reason, we are warranted to infer that, as applied to future punishment, *aionios* is used in the non-absolute sense. That *aionios* is frequently employed in Scripture to express limited duration cannot be denied. It is so used when it is applied to the mountains and the land of Canaan; also where it is connected with the covenant of circumcision and the law of the Passover, unless, indeed, it be held with the Jews that no alteration can happen to the Ceremonial Law, since God himself has declared that it shall last for ever. So far, indeed, is this word from signifying a necessary perpetuity, that it is even applied to those things which have a very short duration, as "He shall serve him for ever" (Ex. xxi: 6); that is, as the Jews themselves expound, to the next Jubilee, whether it were near or far off. Just in the same sense Samuel is said to abide before the Lord "for ever." In the reduplicated form a certain emphasis only is given without any material change of signification. In this double form it is frequently used in quite a limited sense (Isa. x: 8; Jer. vii: 7; xxv: 5). In the New Testament also the word "eternal" is used in a limited sense, as when Sodom and Gomorrah are said to be "set forth, suffering the vengeance of eternal fire"; and when the throne of Christ is said to be for ever and ever (Heb. i: 8), though it must end when "he shall deliver up the kingdom to God." The endless perpetuity of future punishment, as founded upon the statement of our Lord concerning the fire that shall not be quenched, and the worm that dieth not, is explained by the statement in Leviticus, where it is said that the fire burning upon the altar shall "*never* go out"; yet this fire has gone out, for the Messiah caused the sacrifice and the oblation to cease. Again, fire to consume Jerusalem (Ez. xx: 48) which shall not be quenched, is threatened; yet this fire has ceased, and Jerusalem is at this moment inhabited. The expression, "the smoke of their torment ascendeth up for ever and ever," is clearly a metaphor expressive of limited duration. For the substance from which it is evolved burns; and we can not conceive that any substance can burn without loss of parts, which here are perpetually ascending, and "where no wood is there the fire goeth out." This same metaphor, as employed by Isaiah, is clearly subject to the limitation above specified, where, speaking of the judgments of God upon a certain people, it is declared that the fire, the instrument of punishment, "shall not be quenched, night or day"; "the smoke thereof shall go up for ever." Yet, subsequently, it is intimated that the wild beasts and birds of the forest shall possess it "for ever."

When, therefore, it is considered that this term *aionios*, translated "eternal" or "everlasting," is commonly used in Scripture to express limited duration merely, it is all but certain that when employed in the New Testament with reference to the realities of the Christian ages or times, called in Rom. xvi: 25, *"æonian times"* (in Authorized Version, "since the world began"*), *aionios* is to be interpreted in its usual limited import. In the New Testament, however, *aionios* as connected with the Christian ages or *æons* becomes slightly modified in meaning. The element of time drops out of sight, and its significance as an epithet is found in the character of the ages with which it connects its substantive. Thus *æonian* punishment is the punishment distinctive of the Christian ages. In like manner, *æonian* life is the life of ages, the *æonian* God (Rom. xvi: 26) is the God of ages, the *æonian* Spirit (Heb. ix: 14) is the Spirit of ages. There are, then, but two senses in which this term is clearly used in Scripture; it is used in the sense of age-long, and it is used to express connection with the Christian *æons*. If, then, the word *æon* is not used in Scripture, nor anywhere else, in the sense of endlessness, but always denotes a period of time (otherwise, how could Scripture speak of *æons* and *æons* of *æons?*), neither is *æonian* used in that sense. Hence the doctrine of endless punishment has no ground in Scripture; for the *æonian* punishment, whether understood in the sense of age-long, or punishment of or pertaining to the ages, is no more endless than are the ages to which it pertains. This series of *æons*, with their varied phases of special reward and punishment, which, according to the New Testament, precede and prepare men for the final state, must end before Christ can deliver up his kingdom. Thus the æonion reward and punishment are clearly connected with the Kingdom of Christ in its present and future manifestations, æonian life being the life of the ages, and æonian punishment the punishment of the ages, viz., the Christian ages. In accordance with this view, we read (II. Tim. i: 9) of grace given us in Christ before the foundation of the world (times of the ages), and of the end of the times (Heb. ix. 26) or meeting-point of the ages. Also, in I. Cor. x: 11, we have the expression $\tau\acute{\eta}\lambda\eta$ $\tau\tilde{\omega}\nu$ $\alpha\grave{\iota}\acute{\omega}\nu\omega\nu$ ends of the ages. Thus the æonian times or times of the ages, and the $\alpha\grave{\iota}\tilde{\omega}\nu\epsilon\varsigma$, are identical, and represent periods or epochs of limited duration only. Hence our modern conception of duration, as developed by the Church, entirely misconceives and misrepresents the New Testament doctrine of the ages. Indeed, the Biblical conception of duration throughout is not the modern one—*i. e.*, of time immediately succeeded by eternity-absolute, but of Æon succeding Æon, economy following enconomy, until the final Divine order is firmly established.

*Salvator Mundi.

INDEX OF TEXTS.

OLD TESTAMENT.

Page.

Genesis, iii : 22.................... 10
 vi : 3, 4.............10, 14
 vi : 4......................... 74
 ix : 12, 16.......10, 69, 74
 xiii : 15..10, 69, 73, 74, 78
 xvii : 7, 8, 13, 19..12, 69
 ....70, 72, 73, 75, 77
 xxi : 33..............15, 72, 78
 xxix : 3....................143
 xlviii : 4......73, 75, 77, 78
 xlix : 26...........73, 77, 78

Exodus iii : 11..................... 18
 iii : 15......................... 78
 xii : 14, 17, 24...69, 75, 80
 xiv : 13......................... 78
 xv : 18.......71, 75, 76, 99
 xix : 9........................... 69
 xxi : 2........................134
 xxi : 6..12, 70, 134, 140,
 ....142, 143, 169
 xxvii : 21....................... 69
 xxviii : 43...................... 69
 xxix : 9, 28..............69, 80
 xxx : 21......................... 69
 xxxi : 16, 17...........69, 72
 xxxii : 13..............69, 73
 xl : 15.....15, 69, 70, 75, 77,
 ....78, 80

Levit. iii : 17..............69, 80
 vi : 13, 18, 22...........69, 80
 vii : 34, 36................... 69
 x : 15............................. 69
 xvi : 29, 31, 34..69, 73, 75, 77,
78
 xvi................................. 78
 xvii : 7, 11..................... 69
 xxiii : 14, 31, 41........... 69
 xxiv : 3, 8, 9............69, 75
 xxv : 10, 39, 41, 46...67, 73,
 ....75, 134, 142
 xxvi......................108

Deut. xv : 17 ......15, 67, 73, 78, 80,
142
 xxiii : 3, 6...................... 80
 xxxii : 7......................... 67
 xxxii : 40............143, 144

Numb. x : 8........ ......69, 75, 78
 xv : 15........................... 69
 xviii : 8, 11, 19, 23..69, 78, 80
 xix : 10, 21.................... 69
 xxv : 13....69, 72, 73, 75, 77,
78

Joshua iv : 7........... ..69, 77, 78
 xiv : 9..............69, 78, 80

I. Sam. i : 22........... ...76, 78, 83
 ii : 30........................... 15
 vi : 9 143
 vii : 22 143

Page.

I. Sam. xiii : 13.................... 69
 xxvii : 12..................... 78

II. Sam. vii : 13, 16, 24, 25, 26, 29..
 ....,..........68, 69
 xii : 10.......................... 77
 xxii : 51........................ 69
 xxiii : 5........................ 69

I. Kings i : 31 ....15, 78
 ii : 33, 45................68, 69
 viii : 13..............78, 80
 ix : 3, 5.........68, 69, 78
 x : 9, 10...................... 69

II. Kings v : 27........73, 77, 78, 80
 xxi : 7......................... 69

I. Chron. xv : 2................... 69
 xvi : 17......................... 69
 xvii : 12, 14, 22, 23, 27..68,
 ....69, 75
 xxii : 10........................ 69
 xxiii : 13, 25.........69, 78
 xxviii : 4, 7, 8 ....68, 69, 78

II. Chron. ii : 4................... 69
 vii : 3, 16..... 69
 ix : 8.......................... 69
 xiii : 5......................... 68
 xxx : 8........................ 69
 xxxiii : 4..................... 69

Judges ii : 1....................... 69

Job v...........................108
 xii : 12......... 78
 xl : 4........................... 78
 xlii : 4......................... 80

Psalms ix : 5...................... 81
 xviii : 50...................... 69
 xxi : 4.......................... 15
 xxiv : 7........................ 77
 xxv : 6.......................... 66
 xxxvii : 25, 29.......78, 142
 xliv : 25...................... 82
 xlviii : 8, 14..67, 69, 73, 78,
99
 lxxiii : 12......... 67
 lxxvii : 5, 7............15, 69
 lxxviii : 66.................. 81
 lxxxviii : 13, 69.......17, 78
 lxxxix : 3, 4...20, 36, 37, 67,
 ....68, 69
 xc : 2........................... 15
 cii : 28........................ 69
 civ : 5.......................... 78
 cv : 8........................... 69
 cx : 4..................67, 142
 cxi : 9.......................142
 cxii : 6......... ....78, 81
 c..iv : 2, 21..... 99
 cxix : 43, 44, 52..67, 66, 76,
99,

Page.

cxix : 67, 71, 75,.........108
cxxxii : 12......... 69
cxxxvi : 8................. 78
cxxxvi : 17..............143
cxliii : 3.................15, 67
cxlv : 13................. 15
cxlviii : 4, 6.......76, 77, 99

Eccl. i:4................15, 78, 140
 i : 10................. 66
 iii : 11..............12, 15
 xii : 5................. 15

Prov. iii : 11, 12 108
 viii : 23................ 66
 x : 7................. 81
 xxii : 28... ....69, 72
 xxiii : 10................ 69

Isaiah ix : 7...... 67
 x : 8.....................169
 xiii : 20................ 69
 xxiii : 7................ 69
 xxiii : 20................ 69
 xxiv : 5................ 69
 xxiv : 9, 10.... 69
 xxiv : 12.................142
 xxv : 6...... 117
 xxv : 12.................. 82
 xxvi : 4.................133
 xxvi : 5.................. 82
 xxx : 8.................. 77
 xxx : 29.................133
 xxxiii : 14, 20.....69, 80, 81
 xxxiv : 10..69, 73, 75, 77, 81,
142
 xl : 4................ 84
 xl : 28................ 78
 xlvi : 9................ 66
 li : 9, 10................15, 67
 li : 11................ 78
 liv : 8.............70, 78
 lv : 3, 13 78
 lvi : 5................ 78
 lvi : 24................136
 lviii : 12.............69, 74
 lix : 21................ 67
 lx : 15, 19.........76, 78
 lxi : 4................ 69
 lxi : 7................ 78
 lxiii : 11 69
 lxiii : 12................ 78
 lxiv : 4..............12, 66

Jer. ii : 19.....................108
 ii : 20..................... 66
 v : 22..................... 70
 vi : 16..................... 69

Page.

vii : 7...... 69, 73, 77, 142, 169
xvii : 4, 25....69, 73, 77, 78, 81
xviii. 15, 16.........69, 70, 74
xx : 11.............. ......70, 82
xxii : 15, 40.............69, 75
xxiii : 39, 40......70, 81, 83, 84
xxv : 5, 9, 12...70, 77, 142, 169
xxviii. 8...................... 66
xxxi : 40...............69, 73, 78
xxxi : 49.................. 69
xxxii : 40........ 75
xlviii : 47.................. 81
xlix : 6.................. 81
li : 39, 57.................15, 70
lxvi : 24.....................136

Lam. iii : 6.................. 67
 iii : 31, 33.................108
 v : 19.................. 76

Ezek. xvi : 60.................. 69
 xxvi : 20.................67, 69
 xxvi : 25.................142
 xxvii : 26, 28.............'69
 xxxv : 5, 9................ 70
 xxxvi : 2................ 70
 xxxvii : 25.....68, 69, 78, 142
 xxxvii : 26.............69, 78
 xliii : 7.................. 69

Hos. xiii : 14.................117

Dan. ii : 4.................. 77
 ii : 44.............67, 77, 78, 82
 vii : 18.................. 99
 vii : 27.................. 78
 ix : 24.................. 78
 xii : 2....................82, 118
 xii : 3, 7.......71, 75, 82, 99

Nehe. ii : 3..................... 78

Joel ii : 26, 27 ....76, 77
 iii : 20.................69, 142

Micah ii : 9.................. 70
 iv : 5.........11, 71, 76, 79
 —— vii : 14 67

Amos i : 3...................... 69
 i : 11... 69
 ix : 11.................. 67

Jonah ii : 6......9, 70, 72, 73, 75, 78

Hab. iii : 6..9, 72, 73, 75, 77, 78, 84,
116

Nahum iii : 10...................143

Mal. i : 4................... ... 82
 iii : 2, 3 ....111, 135
 iii : 4... 67

APOCRYPHA.

Page.

Wisdom iii : 11...................110
 xvi : 1...................110

Page.

I. Macc. vii : 7...................110

NEW TESTAMENT.

Page.

Matthew vi: 13 ....100, 102
      vii: 33 35
      x: 30....................102
      xii: 22, 39, 40, 49.....100,
     133
      xii: 32.. 93, 104, 132, 134
      xiii: 22, 39, 40, 49,.... 93,
      ....95-7, 133, 134
      xiii: 30, 32......100, 134
      xvi: 6.................. 90
      xviii: 8 ....104, 135
      xviii: 20 25
      xix: 16, 19 ....94, 147
      xix: 29.................128
      xxi: 19....94, 100, 140
      xxii: 22................167
      xxiv: 3..93,100, 102, 133,
     134
      xxiv: 3, 27, 30, 37, 39,
      42, 46, 48, 50......108,
      ....109, 133
      xxiv: 4 ....97, 108
      xxiv: 6, 15, 20, 33, 34..
      ....108, 109
      xxiv: 15, 16............82
      xxv: 6, 10, 13, 19, 27, 31..
     108
      xxv: 32, 33 115
      xxv: 34, 45............106
      xxv: 41, 46..94, 101, 104,
      106, 124, 125, 126, 128,
      ....135, 147, 148, 154
      xxv: 46......81, 89, 94,
      102, 106, 113, 114, 118,
     119
      xxviii: 20..93, 100, 102
Mark iii: 29................104, 132
      iv: 19.........93, 100, 102
      vii: 9..................167
      ix: 43-48 ....114, 136, 137
      x: 17, 30.........94, 100, 102,
      ....128, 147
      xi: 14.......94, 100, 103, 140
      xii....................167
      xiii: 1, 34................109
      xv: 8 25
Luke i: 33 ....92, 95, 100, 102,
      ....140, 142, 144
      i: 55 100
      i: 70 ......93, 95, 98, 100, 133
      x: 25................... 94
      xii: 10.................132
      xvi: 8.........93, 95, 100
      xvi: 9.................. 94
      xviii: 18, 30.....94, 100, 128,
     147
      xx: 34, 35.........93, 99, 100
      xx.....................167
      xx: 36 117
      xxi: 5, 7 109
      xxi: 20, 21.............82
      xxi: 25, 32.............109
John iii: 15, 16, 36...94, 127, 128,
     147
      iv: 14, 36....94, 100, 102, 140

Page.

John v: 21, 29 83
      v: 24, 39.........94, 117, 129
      vi: 33, 34, 53 ....127, 128
      vi: 27, 40, 47, 51, 54, 68...94,
      ...... 100, 103, 127, 140
      vii: 33 25
      viii: 35, 51, 52 ....94, 95, 100,
      ....103, 144
      viii: 47 ....25, 103, 144
      ix: 25.................. 25
      ix: 32....93, 95, 96, 98, 100,
      ....102, 140
      x: 28........ 94, 100, 127, 140
      xi: 26.............94, 100
      xii: 25, 50............94, 128
      xii: 34.... 95, 100, 103, 144
      xiii: 8.......94, 100, 103, 140
      xiv: 16..... 95, 100, 103, 140
      xiv: 19.................127
      xiv: 50 ....12, 127
      xv: 12 143
      xvii: 1, 2 126
      xvii: 2.............94, 128
      xvii: 3.................127
      xvii: 5.................117
      xviii: 37 25
Acts iii: 21 ....93, 98, 100, 133
      iv: 21 ....111, 113
      vi: 10.............52, 123, 124
      vii: 51................. 25
      xiii: 46................147
      xv: 18............ 93, 98, 100
Romans i: 20 ....122, 123, 164
      i: 23 ....120, 123
      i: 25 ....95, 100
      ii: 7 ....94, 120, 124
      v: 21 ....94, 128
      vi: 22, 23 94
      ix: 5.............. 95, 101
      xi: 25, 26.............. 75
      xi: 36.............95, 101
      xii: 2......15, 93, 100, 102
      xv: 25................. 96
      xvi: 25.........94, 117, 170
      xvi: 26.........117, 170
      xvi: 26, 27.........95, 101
I. Cor. i: 20..................100
      ii: 6, 7, 8 ....93, 100
      ii: 7........... 100, 102, 133
      iii: 18.............93, 100
      v: 5...................137
      viii: 13.... 94, 100, 140, 143
      ix: 1................... 25
      ix: 25 ....120, 123
      x: 11......93, 97, 100, 102,
      .... 133, 134, 170
      xi: 31.................101
      xv.........67, 117, 119, 135
      xv: 22.............67, 117
      xv: 24, 28.........92, 144
      xv: 28.............95, 144
      xv: 42, 50 ....120, 123
      xv: 51, 54.....120, 122, 123
      xv: 52..................123

Page.

II. Cor. iv : 2 25
 iv : 4................93, 100
 iv : 17................94, 99
 iv : 18...................95
 v : 1...................95
 vi : 10...................25
 ix : 9................95, 100
 xi : 31......93, 95, 101, 102
Gal. i : 4................93, 100
 i : 5.....95, 96, 97, 99, 101, 108
 i : 14...................93
 vi : 8.................... 94
Eph. i : 10................132
 i : 21................93, 100
 ii : 2............93, 100, 102
 ii : 9...................134
 ii : 7....96, 97, 100, 101, 102
 iii : 9, 11..93, 95, 98, 101, 133, 134
 iii : 21..94, 96, 99, 101, 102, 134
 v : 14...................83
 vi : 12...................100
Col. i : 26......... 97, 101, 133, 134
Philip. iv : 20........95, 96, 99, 101
I. Thess. v : 3 137
II. Thess. i : 9...104, 113, 127, 137
 ii : 16.................. 94
I. Tim. i : 4 ....121, 123
 i : 16...................94
 i : 17..95, 96, 99, 101, 102, 120, 122
 v : 6 82
 vi : 9 137
 vi : 12................94, 147
 vi : 16 ....120, 124
 vi : 17...............96, 100
II. Tim. i 9.............94, 97, 133
 i : 10 .... 120, 124
 ii : 10 95
 iv : 10...............94, 100
 iv : 18...... 95, 96, 99, 101
Titus i : 2 ....94, 133
 i : 12.................25
 ii : 12.................94, 100
 iii : 7...................94
Philemon 15.................... 94
Hebrews i : 2...........94, 100, 102
 i : 8.............96, 99, 101
 ii : 12.................15
 iii : 1. 10.................25
 v : 6.................100, 140
 v : 9...................94
 vi : 2......... 95, 104, 138
 vi : 4...................129
 vi : 5.................100, 140
 vi : 6...................134
 vi : 20........92, 100, 140
 vii : 6...................119

Page.

Hebrews vii : 11, 12 15
 vii : 15, 16......... 122, 123
 vii : 16......119, 121, 122
 vii : 17, 21, 24, 28..92, 95, 100, 140
 ix : 12, 14, 15.......... 95
 ix : 23...................133
 ix : 26.... 94, 97, 100, 133, 134, 170
 x : 29.................114
 xi : 3.................94, 100
 xii : 5...................107
 xii : 9...................135
 xii : 28...................135
 xiii : 8, 21....95, 96, 101
 xiii : 20...................95
 xvii : 21................... 92
I. Pet. i : 3, 4 ....119, 122, 123
 i : 23 ....100, 123
 i : 25...................95
 iii : 15...................25
 iii : 18, 20 ....92, 138
 iv : 11.......92, 95, 99, 101
 v : 4...99, 101, 119, 120, 123
 v : 10, 11 ....95, 99, 101
II. Pet. i : 11 92
 i : 12...................25
 i : 17........104, 137, 138
 ii : 9..............111, 113
 iii : 18...........92, 95, 100
Jude 6 ....122, 164
 7............. 35, 104, 135, 165
 13............104, 137, 138
 21 94
 25 95
I. John i : 2.................... 94
 ii : 15...................15
 ii : 17.................95, 100
 ii : 25...................94
 iii : 15...............94, 128
 iv : 18........111, 113, 114
 v : 11, 13, 20 ....94, 128
II. John, 2 ....95, 100
Rev. i : 6 ....92, 96, 101
 i : 18.................95, 99, 101
 iii : 1...................82
 iv : 9, 10....95, 96, 99, 101, 102
 v : 13, 14... 95, 96, 99, 101
 vii : 12...........95, 96, 99, 101
 x : 6.............95, 99, 101
 xi : 15...........92, 99, 101
 xiv : 6...................93
 xiv : 11...96, 99, 101, 104, 139
 xv : 7.........95, 96, 99, 101
 xviii : 3.................143
 xix : 3.........99, 101, 104, 139
 xx : 10.. 96, 99, 101, 104, 133, 139, 142, 143, 147
 xxi : 4...................111
 xxii : 5.............95, 99, 101

www.ingramcontent.com/pod-product-compliance
Lightning Source LLC
Chambersburg PA
CBHW031114020726
47495CB00007B/2202